T0275179

# Sephardic Israeli Cuisine:

## A Mediterranean Mosaic

# THE HIPPOCRENE
# COOKBOOK LIBRARY

## Africa and Oceania
Best of Regional African Cooking
Traditional South African Cookery
Taste of Eritrea
Good Food from Australia

## Asia and Middle East
The Best of Taiwanese Cuisine
Imperial Mongolian Cooking
The Best of Regional Thai Cuisine
Japanese Home Cooking
The Best of Korean Cuisine
Egyptian Cooking
Sephardic Israeli Cuisine
Healthy South Indian Cooking
The Indian Spice Kitchen
Best of Kashmiri Cooking
The Cuisine of the Caucasus Mountains
Afghan Food and Cookery
The Art of Persian Cooking
The Art of Turkish Cooking
The Art of Uzbek Cooking

## Mediterranean
Best of Greek Cuisine, Expanded Edition
Taste of Malta
A Spanish Family Cookbook
Tastes of North Africa

## Western Europe
Art of Dutch Cooking, Expanded Edition
A Belgian Cookbook
Cooking in the French Fashion (bilingual)
Cuisines of Portuguese Encounters
The Swiss Cookbook
The Art of Irish Cooking
Feasting Galore Irish-Style
Traditional Food from Scotland
Traditional Food from Wales
The Scottish-Irish Pub and Hearth Cookbook
A Treasury of Italian Cuisine (bilingual)

## Scandinavia
Best of Scandinavian Cooking
The Best of Finnish Cooking
The Best of Smorgasbord Cooking
Good Food from Sweden
Tastes & Tales of Norway
Icelandic Food & Cookery

## Central Europe
All Along the Rhine
All Along the Danube
Bavarian Cooking
Best of Austrian Cuisine
The Best of Czech Cooking
The Best of Slovak Cooking
The Art of Hungarian Cooking
Hungarian Cookbook
Polish Heritage Cookery
The Best of Polish Cooking
Old Warsaw Cookbook
Old Polish Traditions
Treasury of Polish Cuisine (bilingual)
Poland's Gourmet Cuisine
The Polish Country Kitchen Cookbook

## Eastern Europe
Art of Lithuanian Cooking
Best of Albanian Cooking
Traditional Bulgarian Cooking
Best of Croatian Cooking
Taste of Romania
Taste of Latvia
The Best of Russian Cooking
The Best of Ukrainian Cuisine

## Americas
Argentina Cooks
A Taste of Haiti
A Taste of Quebec
Cooking With Cajun Women
Cooking the Caribbean Way
French Caribbean Cuisine
Mayan Cooking
The Honey Cookbook
The Art of Brazilian Cookery
The Art of South American Cookery
Old Havana Cookbook (bilingual)

# Sephardic Israeli Cuisine:

## A Mediterranean Mosaic

SHEILAH KAUFMAN

HIPPOCRENE BOOKS, INC.
NEW YORK

Cover photograph by Dalia Carmel
Inside photographs by Vivienne Roumani-Denn,
Dalia Carmel, and Sheilah Kaufman
Author photograph by Lee Van Grack


Book and jacket design by Acme Klong Design, Inc.

For more information, address;
HIPPOCRENE BOOKS, INC.
171 Madison Avenue
New York, NY 10016

ISBN: 978-0-7818-1310-5

Cataloging-in-Publication Data available from the Library of Congress.
Printed in the United States of America.

# DEDICATION

With much appreciation and thanks to my many new friends, especially Viviane, Daniela, Leah, Judith, and Lydia; Randall Bel Inante and Vivienne Roumani-Denn of the American Sephardi Federation in New York, and all the others who contributed recipes and helped with this book. Thanks to my family and friends for testing my recipes, and my husband Barry for being my computer guru. A big thanks to Connie for letting me use her extensive library; an extra big thanks to my longtime friend Ginnie Manuel, an excellent word craftsperson; and to Dalia Carmel for her help, photos, and friendship.

*Sephardic Israeli Cuisine*

# HYMN BENDIGAMOS

The Hymn Bendigamos is the grace after meals, according to the *Custom of the Spanish and Portuguese Jews*, edited and translated by David de Sola Pool and published by the Union of Sephardic Congregations, 8 West 70th Street, New York, NY 10023. The following is a translation my friend Vivienne found and shared with me.

Let us bless the Most High
The Lord who created us,
Let us give him thanks
For the good things which he has given us.

Praised be his Holy Name,
Because he always took pity on us.
Praise the Lord, for he is good,
For his mercy is everlasting.

Let us bless the Most High
Firstly for his Law,
Which binds our race
With heaven continually,
Praised be his Holy Name,
Because he always took pity on us.

Praise the Lord, for he is good,
For his mercy is everlasting.
Let us bless the Most High,
Secondly for the bread
And also for the foods
Which we have eaten together.
For we eat and drink joyfully
His mercy has never failed us.

Praise the Lord, for he is good,
For his mercy is everlasting.

Blessed be this house,
The home of his presence,
Where we keep his feast,
With happiness and permanence.

Praised be his Holy Name,
Because he always took pity on us.
Praise the Lord, for he is good,
For his mercy is everlasting.

# CONTENTS

INTRODUCTION . . . . . . . . . . . . . . . . . . . . . . . . . . . . . 11

A BRIEF HISTORY OF THE JEWS
AND THEIR WANDERINGS . . . . . . . . . . . . . . . . . . 15

JEWISH CUISINE . . . . . . . . . . . . . . . . . . . . . . . . . . . 21

KASHRUT: WHAT IS KOSHER? . . . . . . . . . . . . . . . 25

JEWISH HOLIDAYS . . . . . . . . . . . . . . . . . . . . . . . . . 27

TERMS USED IN THIS BOOK . . . . . . . . . . . . . . . . . 37

CONDIMENTS AND SPICES . . . . . . . . . . . . . . . . . 41
  Baharat . . . . . . . . . . . . . . . . . . . . . . . . . . . . . . . . 43
  Hawayij . . . . . . . . . . . . . . . . . . . . . . . . . . . . . . . 44
  Hilbeh . . . . . . . . . . . . . . . . . . . . . . . . . . . . . . . . 45
  Hulba . . . . . . . . . . . . . . . . . . . . . . . . . . . . . . . . . 46
  Seven Spice Mixture . . . . . . . . . . . . . . . . . . . . . . 47
  Za'atar . . . . . . . . . . . . . . . . . . . . . . . . . . . . . . . . 48
  Zhoug . . . . . . . . . . . . . . . . . . . . . . . . . . . . . . . . 49
  Preserved Lemons . . . . . . . . . . . . . . . . . . . . . . . 50
  Tahina Sauce . . . . . . . . . . . . . . . . . . . . . . . . . . . 51
  Strained Yogurt . . . . . . . . . . . . . . . . . . . . . . . . . 52
  Yogurt Cheese . . . . . . . . . . . . . . . . . . . . . . . . . . 53

MEZZE (Appetizers, Snacks, and Starters) . . . . . . . . . . 55
  Cheese Ball with Walnuts . . . . . . . . . . . . . . . . . . 56
  Crescent Olive Puffs . . . . . . . . . . . . . . . . . . . . . 57
  Eggplant with Tahini . . . . . . . . . . . . . . . . . . . . . 59
  Fava Beans . . . . . . . . . . . . . . . . . . . . . . . . . . . . . 60
  Fish Roe Spread/Salad . . . . . . . . . . . . . . . . . . . . 61
  Hummus . . . . . . . . . . . . . . . . . . . . . . . . . . . . . . 62
  Tomato Spread . . . . . . . . . . . . . . . . . . . . . . . . . 64

Stuffed Grape Leaves . . . . . . . . . . . . . . . . . . . . . . . 64
Walnut Dip . . . . . . . . . . . . . . . . . . . . . . . . . . . . . . 66
Yogurt and Cucumber Spread/Salad. . . . . . . . . . . . . . 67

SOUPS. . . . . . . . . . . . . . . . . . . . . . . . . . . . . . . . . . . 69
Cold Yogurt Soup . . . . . . . . . . . . . . . . . . . . . . . . . 71
Cucumber with Yogurt Soup . . . . . . . . . . . . . . . . . . 72
Egyptian Green Herb Soup . . . . . . . . . . . . . . . . . . . 73
Fava Bean Soup. . . . . . . . . . . . . . . . . . . . . . . . . . . 75
Harira . . . . . . . . . . . . . . . . . . . . . . . . . . . . . . . . . 77
Lemon Chicken Soup . . . . . . . . . . . . . . . . . . . . . . . 79
Red Lentil Soup . . . . . . . . . . . . . . . . . . . . . . . . . . 81
Tamar's Yemenite Chicken Soup. . . . . . . . . . . . . . . . 82

SALADS. . . . . . . . . . . . . . . . . . . . . . . . . . . . . . . . . . 85
Carrot and Orange Salad . . . . . . . . . . . . . . . . . . . . 87
Doreen's Fattoush Salad. . . . . . . . . . . . . . . . . . . . . 88
Jerusalem Tahini Salad . . . . . . . . . . . . . . . . . . . . . 89
Tabouleh . . . . . . . . . . . . . . . . . . . . . . . . . . . . . . . 90

CHICKEN. . . . . . . . . . . . . . . . . . . . . . . . . . . . . . . . . 93
Chicken Pie . . . . . . . . . . . . . . . . . . . . . . . . . . . . . 95
Chicken Breasts with Kumquats. . . . . . . . . . . . . . . . 98
Chicken Hamin. . . . . . . . . . . . . . . . . . . . . . . . . . . 99
Chicken with Okra . . . . . . . . . . . . . . . . . . . . . . . . 100
Chicken with Olives . . . . . . . . . . . . . . . . . . . . . . . 102
Circassian Chicken . . . . . . . . . . . . . . . . . . . . . . . . 103
Grandma's Chicken Meatballs . . . . . . . . . . . . . . . . . 105
Mediterranean Chicken. . . . . . . . . . . . . . . . . . . . . . 107

FISH. . . . . . . . . . . . . . . . . . . . . . . . . . . . . . . . . . . . 109
David Dahan's Moroccan Fish with Ancho Chilies . . . 111
Fish Stuffed with Dates. . . . . . . . . . . . . . . . . . . . . . 112
Grilled Fish with Chermoula . . . . . . . . . . . . . . . . . . 113
Leah Perez's Mediterranean Fish Bake . . . . . . . . . . . 114
Lydia Wolf's Fish with Tomato Sauce and Peppers . . . 115
Spicy Fish. . . . . . . . . . . . . . . . . . . . . . . . . . . . . . . 116

Walnut Stuffed Fish . . . . . . . . . . . . . . . . . . . . . . . . . . 117

MEAT . . . . . . . . . . . . . . . . . . . . . . . . . . . . . . . . . . . . . 119
   Beans With Meat and Spinach . . . . . . . . . . . . . . . . . 121
   Couscous Tagine . . . . . . . . . . . . . . . . . . . . . . . . . . . 122
   Daniela Sciaky's Spinach-Wrapped Meatballs . . . . . . . 124
   Lamb Pies . . . . . . . . . . . . . . . . . . . . . . . . . . . . . . . 125
   Mafrum . . . . . . . . . . . . . . . . . . . . . . . . . . . . . . . . . 127
   Meatballs in Dough . . . . . . . . . . . . . . . . . . . . . . . . . 129
   Meat and Eggplant Pie . . . . . . . . . . . . . . . . . . . . . . 132
   Moroccan Cholent . . . . . . . . . . . . . . . . . . . . . . . . . . 134
   Sephardic Stuffed Cabbage . . . . . . . . . . . . . . . . . . . 136

MEATLESS, EGG, AND CHEESE DISHES . . . . . . . . 139
   Brown Hard-Cooked Eggs . . . . . . . . . . . . . . . . . . . . 141
   Chickpeas and Rice . . . . . . . . . . . . . . . . . . . . . . . . . 142
   Cilantro Pancakes . . . . . . . . . . . . . . . . . . . . . . . . . . 143
   Cilantro Chutney . . . . . . . . . . . . . . . . . . . . . . . . . . 145
   Eggplant with Tomato Sauce . . . . . . . . . . . . . . . . . . 146
   Individual Stuffed Pies . . . . . . . . . . . . . . . . . . . . . . 148
   Fillings: Spinach, Potato, Pumpkin, Cheese . . . . . . . 149
   Quick Boyos . . . . . . . . . . . . . . . . . . . . . . . . . . . . . 151
   Potato and Leek Patties . . . . . . . . . . . . . . . . . . . . . 152
   Shou Shou's Fresh Herb KuKu . . . . . . . . . . . . . . . . 154
   Uli's Falafel . . . . . . . . . . . . . . . . . . . . . . . . . . . . . . 156

VEGETABLES . . . . . . . . . . . . . . . . . . . . . . . . . . . . . . 159
   Fava Beans with Lemon and Garlic . . . . . . . . . . . . . 161
   Moroccan Sweet Carrots . . . . . . . . . . . . . . . . . . . . . 163
   Okra . . . . . . . . . . . . . . . . . . . . . . . . . . . . . . . . . . . 164
   Spinach Bake . . . . . . . . . . . . . . . . . . . . . . . . . . . . 165
   Sweet Couscous . . . . . . . . . . . . . . . . . . . . . . . . . . 166
   Sweet Rice with Nuts . . . . . . . . . . . . . . . . . . . . . . . 167
   Zucchini with Sauce . . . . . . . . . . . . . . . . . . . . . . . . 168

BREADS . . . . . . . . . . . . . . . . . . . . . . . . . . . . . . . . . . . 171
   Basic Pita . . . . . . . . . . . . . . . . . . . . . . . . . . . . . . . 173

Flat Bread . . . . . . . . . . . . . . . . . . . . . . . . . . . . . 174
Jackie Ben Efraim's Challah . . . . . . . . . . . . . . . . . . . 175
Lebanese Bread . . . . . . . . . . . . . . . . . . . . . . . . . . 177
Matzo . . . . . . . . . . . . . . . . . . . . . . . . . . . . . . . . 179
Yemenite Sweet Sabbath Bread  . . . . . . . . . . . . . . . . 180

DESSERTS . . . . . . . . . . . . . . . . . . . . . . . . . . . . . 183
Almond Macaroons  . . . . . . . . . . . . . . . . . . . . . . . 185
Baklava . . . . . . . . . . . . . . . . . . . . . . . . . . . . . . . 186
Butter Cookies . . . . . . . . . . . . . . . . . . . . . . . . . . 188
Butter Ring Cookies . . . . . . . . . . . . . . . . . . . . . . . 189
Chocolate Salami . . . . . . . . . . . . . . . . . . . . . . . . . 190
Coconut Macaroons . . . . . . . . . . . . . . . . . . . . . . . 191
Dates in Pastry . . . . . . . . . . . . . . . . . . . . . . . . . . 192
Hanukah Doughnuts . . . . . . . . . . . . . . . . . . . . . . . 194
Lemon Cake . . . . . . . . . . . . . . . . . . . . . . . . . . . . 196
Lemon Sherbet . . . . . . . . . . . . . . . . . . . . . . . . . . 198
Marzipan . . . . . . . . . . . . . . . . . . . . . . . . . . . . . . 199
Orange Walnut Cake . . . . . . . . . . . . . . . . . . . . . . . 200
Pretzel-Shaped Cookies . . . . . . . . . . . . . . . . . . . . . 202
Purim Roses . . . . . . . . . . . . . . . . . . . . . . . . . . . . 204
Rice Pudding . . . . . . . . . . . . . . . . . . . . . . . . . . . 206
Sesame Brittle . . . . . . . . . . . . . . . . . . . . . . . . . . . 207
Nut Cake with Sugar Syrup . . . . . . . . . . . . . . . . . . . 208

SEPHARDIC PASSOVER . . . . . . . . . . . . . . . . . . . . 211
Fish in Salsa . . . . . . . . . . . . . . . . . . . . . . . . . . . . 213
Haroset from Turkey . . . . . . . . . . . . . . . . . . . . . . . 214
Haroset of the Abravanel Family . . . . . . . . . . . . . . . . 215
Meat and Leek Patties . . . . . . . . . . . . . . . . . . . . . . 217
Moroccan Spicy Apricot Lamb Shanks . . . . . . . . . . . . 219
Moroccan Sweet Potato Cake . . . . . . . . . . . . . . . . . . 221
Passover Breakfast Fritters  . . . . . . . . . . . . . . . . . . . 223
Passover Fava Bean Soup . . . . . . . . . . . . . . . . . . . . 224
Passover Spinach Bake  . . . . . . . . . . . . . . . . . . . . . 226
Passover Sponge Cake . . . . . . . . . . . . . . . . . . . . . . 227

ASHKENAZIC CONTRIBUTIONS. . . . . . . . . . . . . 229
   Babka. . . . . . . . . . . . . . . . . . . . . . . . . . . . . . . . . 231
   Blintzes . . . . . . . . . . . . . . . . . . . . . . . . . . . . . . . 233
   Cholent . . . . . . . . . . . . . . . . . . . . . . . . . . . . . . . 235
   Cold Beet Borscht . . . . . . . . . . . . . . . . . . . . . . . 237
   Connie's Stuffed Cabbage. . . . . . . . . . . . . . . . . . 238
   Cornmeal Mush . . . . . . . . . . . . . . . . . . . . . . . . . 239
   Herring Salad. . . . . . . . . . . . . . . . . . . . . . . . . . . 241
   Knishes . . . . . . . . . . . . . . . . . . . . . . . . . . . . . . . 242
   Lentil Spread (Mock Chopped Liver) . . . . . . . . . . 244
   Marilyn Bagel's Bagels. . . . . . . . . . . . . . . . . . . . 245
   Mock Stuffed Kishka. . . . . . . . . . . . . . . . . . . . . 247
   Roslyn Wolf's No-Fail Matzo Balls . . . . . . . . . . . 248
   Roggie Weinraub's Mandel Bread. . . . . . . . . . . . 249
   Rugelach . . . . . . . . . . . . . . . . . . . . . . . . . . . . . . 250

BIBLIOGRAPHY . . . . . . . . . . . . . . . . . . . . . . . . . . 253

INDEX. . . . . . . . . . . . . . . . . . . . . . . . . . . . . . . . . . 255

*Sephardic Israeli Cuisine*

# INTRODUCTION

**W**hen I began writing this book, I did not realize how difficult it would be. Israeli cooking is like a giant colorful mosaic or puzzle that I had to take apart to find the components. In the process, I discovered that native Israeli cooking depends on the land of origin of the cook; there is no single Israeli or Sephardic cuisine in the sense that there is a French or Italian cuisine.

A number of years ago, Stephen and Ethel Longstreet wrote a book, *The Joys of Jewish Cooking*, in which they characterized Israeli cooking by noting, "the native cuisine of Israel itself is little better than the food served in the Wild West of the American frontier a hundred years ago." Fortunately for all of us, this observation is no longer valid.

*Druze Coffee Pots*

An article issued by the Office of Public Affairs of the Israeli Embassy begins by admitting, "despite its Biblical association with milk and honey, Israel lacks a long standing culinary heritage. Only a few years ago, Israelis even doubted the existence of their own authentic cuisine. Today, most people agree that there is a distinctive Israeli cuisine, though like the many aspects of the society, it is uniquely multifaceted. It reflects the various communities in the country and their diverse geographical and cultural origins. The Israeli kitchen is home to the multitude of foods and recipes, which have accompanied the Jewish people's return to the 'Land of Milk and Honey.'"

Joan Nathan put it so beautifully in her book *The Flavor of Jerusalem* when she said "Jerusalem cookery remains a rich mixture of tastes rather than a single flavor of a melting pot." In her new book, *The Foods of Israel Today*, she comments that "the founding fathers and mothers of modern Israel had an idea of a melting-pot culinary style...envisioned that the country would have a distinct 'Israeli food'...but 20 years ago they realized that the melting-pot idea wasn't going to work. Now we think of Israeli food as a mosaic within the frame of the nation, where each dish is a different color and stands by itself."

When people talk about "Jewish food," they usually mean the cooking of Eastern European and German (Ashkenazic) Jews. For many, the term also connotes those items they are familiar with from delicatessens—brisket, corned beef, pastrami, bagels, lox, mandel bread. Jewish cooking has been revolutionized in this century by the upheaval that Jewish life experienced with modernization (refrigeration) and the availability of many more and different foods. Today's modern cooks are also more health conscious and turn away from rich, fatty foods with high salt content. More processed and prepared foods, new cooking techniques, and exposure to the cuisines of other cultures have all led to changes in Israeli eating habits. In Israel, many new foods were introduced by the waves of Europeans before and after the Holocaust.

Since biblical times Jews in Israel ate the foods of the land, many of which were mentioned in the Bible. After their expulsion from Spain, Jews came to the Holy Land and brought their cultural and dietary influences, as did other Jews from Greece, Italy, Morocco, Persia, Yemen, Ethiopia, and other countries. Now Israel is home to people from everywhere and thus it is not surprising to find such mass-appeal food items as pizza, Chinese food, and sushi.

There are many differences between Sephardic and Ashkenazic food. Sephardic cuisine includes a wide diversity of spices, seasonings, and flavorings including cinnamon, cloves, sumac, cardamom, hot chili, cumin, fenugreek, turmeric, saffron, almond essence, rose and orange flower water, mastika, coriander, and tahini paste. On the other hand, Ashkenazic recipes employ paprika, dried herbs, dill, parsley, vinegar, and vanilla extract. Both cultures use onions and garlic but Ashkenazic cooks rely heavily on potatoes and cabbage, while Sephardic cooks are more likely to include eggplant, peppers, artichokes, leeks, okra, zucchini, fava beans, olives, and fennel.

For both baking and cooking Ashkenazic grains of choice are wheat, barley and buckwheat. By contrast, Sephardic Jews favor rice, couscous, semolina, and bulgur. The most popular fruits used in Ashekenazic recipes are apples, pears, cherries, and currants. Sephardic recipes make liberal use of melons, apricots, persimmons, oranges, peaches, lemons, limes, figs, and dates.

Interestingly, there is no Arabic word for "dessert." My Sephardic friends have told me that they finish a meal with fruit, not with processed sweets as is more commonplace in America. However, after the meal is over, they adjourn for coffee and cookies or pastries.

Today Israel has developed an authentic food culture, which offers a wealth of colorful, rich, and delicious choices, including foods that came from neighboring Arab cultures. A relatively new phenomenon is the Israeli breakfast. Eating breakfast in Israel can be an unbelievable experience. Many hotels pattern their breakfast buffets after meals served on kibbutzim, where people have put in many hours of work by 8 a.m. The buffet offers a tantalizing variety of Sephardic and Ashkenazic foods. A typical Israeli breakfast buffet can include all types of fresh fruit and juices followed by any or all of the following: pita bread; hard-cooked eggs; different types of herring salads; rolls; Israeli salad; eggplant with tahini; a variety of fish (such as smoked codfish and whitefish, sardines, smoked salmon, mackerel), assorted cheeses; sliced onions and tomatoes; cream cheese; cottage cheese; a variety of yogurts; Labaneh; diverse breads and bagels; and blintzes. No one should ever walk away hungry from breakfast in Israel!

This book is designed to showcase the diversity of influences and flavors that make up Sephardic cooking. Enjoy!

*Sephardic Israeli Cuisine*

# A BRIEF HISTORY OF THE JEWS
# AND THEIR WANDERINGS

From the earliest days of recorded history of the Jewish people through the first century of the Common Era, most of the world's Jews lived in, around, or near Jerusalem (the capital of what is now Israel) because they wanted to be near the Temple. During this period, the Temple was used for worship, as a gathering place, for prayer, and even as a focal point for business and trade.

*Rabbi Rachamim Barda*

In 722 B.C. the Assyrians conquered Israel and dispersed many Jews to Persia and the area near the Caspian Sea. But the Jews weren't really expelled or exiled from Israel until 586 B.C. when the Babylonians destroyed the Temple, enslaved the Jews, and "carried them off" into exile in Babylon (near present day Baghdad). While in Babylonia the Jews managed to retain their culture and identity. They were finally allowed to return to Israel and rebuild the Temple in the sixth century, after the Persians con-quered the Babylonians. By this time, Jews also lived in Syria, Egypt, and Persia. It was during this time of living among the Persians that the foundations of Sephardic culture and cuisine were laid. The Persian dominance lasted until the rule of Alexander the Great. After his death, and until 176 B.C., the Jews became more urbanized due to exposure to Hellenistic cultures.

By 176 B.C. a great number of Jews began to move to such cities as Alexandria and Antioch, along with other communities in Egypt. At that time, Antiochus Epiphanes became king and insti-tuted a policy dictating that everyone in his kingdom, including the Jews, become Hellenized. In 166 B.C. during his reign, the Jews revolted after the king forbade the worship of their God and the custom of circumcision. During the fighting, the Greeks desecrated the Temple by installing Greek gods in it and by sacrificing pigs on its altar. Ultimately the Maccabean revolt was successful, and the Temple was rededicated. This is commemorated in the celebration of Chanukah because of a miracle that happened there (see Chanukah, page 30, for more details).

This same period also saw a steady stream of emigration from Judea to the cities of the Greek Diaspora—not only Alexandria and Antioch, but also Damascus and a host of communities along the western coast of Asia Minor, the Aegean, and in Greece. By the first century B.C., there were Jews in all the cities of the known world, and in 30 B.C., Egypt had been absorbed into the Roman Empire, with about a million Jews in the Nile Valley, the Delta, and Alexandria.

Until A.D. 70, the Jews of Judea (a Roman province with Jerusalem as its capital) were ruled by Rome and lived under Roman law. However, the Jews refused to be assimilated into the Roman way of life. Because they refused to worship Roman pagan gods in the Temple, there were a number of attempts to overthrow the Roman government in Judea. During the summer of A.D. 71, the Roman army laid siege to Jerusalem, captured and burned parts of the city and destroyed the Temple. Jews that were not sold into slavery, exiled, or murdered remained in the area. Jewish life was reorganized and synagogues (houses of gathering/study) were built to help maintain the Jewish identity. Thus, a Jewish way of life continued to exist throughout the Roman Empire.

Over the next few hundred years, Judaism remained a separate minority religion in the Mediterranean countries. The largest Jewish population in this period was located in Babylonia, Persia, and the lands of the Middle East. Jews were also found in smaller numbers in North Africa and Iberia. In addition, a tiny number lived in Italy, France, Sicily, Germany, and in what are today Greece, Bulgaria, and the Balkan Republics. From about the tenth century until the middle of the nineteenth century, there was even a flourishing community of Chinese Jews in the city of K'aifeng-fu, China.

No one is quite sure when the first Jewish settlers arrived in Spain, but it is believed to have been between the time of the first Temple (953 to 586 B.C.) and the first century A.D. By the fourth century, there were a number of Jewish communities throughout Iberia, and they were already beginning to suffer from discrimination. Conditions improved somewhat in A.D. 711 when the Muslim Moors of North Africa crossed the Straits of Gibraltar, conquered Spain, and placed it under Muslim control. Under Muslim rule, the Jews enjoyed a period of toleration and enlightened prosperity. For the next 500 years, called The Golden Age of Spain, these Jews prospered until the notorious Inquisition came to Spain.

*Old aula. Jewish quarter in Spain*

The increased persecution of Jews living in Western Europe actually began at the time of the first Crusade. Many Christians who set out for the Holy Land (to attack the infidels) never got anywhere near Jerusalem and instead slaughtered Jews along the way. By A.D. 1204, which coincided with the fourth Crusade, the Jews suffered greatly from many restrictions that affected their economic and social life (including the "invention" of the ghetto). The year 1391 marked the first time that Jews were expelled from Spain, and the first Sephardic Jews began to arrive in Crete, Constantinople, and Adrianople (part of the new Byzantine Empire). During this time, many Jews from Spain and Hungary also immigrated to the new Ottoman Empire.

Then came the marriage of King Ferdinand II and Queen Isabella, who focused on uniting Spain under one religion: Catholicism. In 1492, Isabella, after conquering the last Moorish king, signed the Alhambra Decree, giving the Jews the choice of converting or leaving Spain forever. The estimates for the number of Jews forced to leave Spain range from 160,000 to 250,000. Many Jews went to Muslim countries in the Ottoman Empire and North Africa, where they were welcomed by the Ottoman Turks. According to Lorraine Gerstl, in her *Jewish Cooking Secrets*, Sultan Mehmet II said, "They say the King of Spain is a wise man. I say he is a fool as he expelled the Jews." The Jews were the teachers, doctors, poets, bankers, and they fueled the commerce of Spain. The Sultan dispatched his own ships to pick up the Jews and transport them to Turkey.

In addition, Salonika (in Greece) became an important Jewish center for the Sephardic Jews. A small number went to Italy and the Netherlands; some went to Portugal for a short time until they were forced to leave and then most moved to Amsterdam. Those Jews who remained in Spain were persecuted after their forced conversions.

At this time, two important Jewish centers emerged in Western Europe—Iberia (called *Sepharad*) and the Rhine River Valley (called *Ashkenaz*). These two medieval Jewish communities were geographically close but were dissimilar in other ways, leading to a gradual development of differences in customs, law, pronunciation of Hebrew, and foods.

In France and Germany, during the Middle Ages, the Jews lived in an alien culinary environment. Their non-Jewish neighbors ate pork and shellfish, used lard, and in cooking, mixed meat and dairy products. The Jews of Central and Eastern Europe became known as *Ashkenazim* (from *Ashkenaz*, meaning Germany), and most can trace their ancestors back to Germany or parts of Central Europe.

The Ashkenazim became resourceful in adapting to the local foods, while those Jews living in Muslim countries had culinary customs that were almost identical to those of their neighbors. As was the case in Jewish law, the Muslim diet forbade the eating of pork, and it used little, if any, dairy products in the preparation of meals. Therefore, the Sephardic Jews were easily able to adopt the foods and recipes of their Muslim neighbors. Borrowing from its earlier Persian heritage, this cuisine included sweet and sour dishes, and combinations of meat and fruit. In time, the Jews of

Spain and Portugal developed a diet that combined Iberian, Arabic, and Jewish cooking styles. This cuisine was much more diverse and sophisticated than that of the medieval French/German Jews. Nonetheless, due to a degree of interaction between the communities, there was some commonality in certain foods.

Besides pronouncing Hebrew differently, the Sephardic Jews and the Ashkenazic Jews have a number of divergent customs and ways of observing the holidays. The Jews who were natives of Middle Eastern countries are referred to as *Hamizrach*—the ethnic communities of the Orient—"Oriental" Jews. These countries include Iran, Iraq, Kurdistan, Armenia, Uzbekistan, Bukhara, Georgia, Azerbaijan, Yemen, Aden, Turkey, Lebanon, Egypt, Syria, Tunisia, Algeria, and part of Morocco. Because a large number of Sephardic Jews lived in the same areas as the Hamizrach, they have more or less blended into those countries where they settled. As a result, even today there remains some confusion as to who is Sephardic and who is Oriental.

*Members of the same family in "European" and traditional garb*

In the realm of cooking, however, all three groups share one key similarity: no matter where they live, their diets conform to the rules of Kashrut, while utilizing whatever ingredients are available from the land and sea. Although the types of foods these three groups consume may be similar, differences in method of preparation arise from unique local customs and ingredients. Regional spices, grains, and vegetables account for variations on basic Jewish dishes. For example, whereas Ashkenazic Jews may use potatoes, barley, and sweet paprika, Sephardic Jews might use rice, chickpeas, and such exotic spices as saffron.

Since its founding in 1948, Israel has become a virtual melting pot for Jews from all over the world. Many were refugees from Hitler's Europe, but others also emigrated from the oppressed communities of Iran, Iraq, Saudi Arabia, Yemen, and North Africa. As a result, Israeli cooking combines elements from both European and Middle Eastern styles, with a strong emphasis on native fruits and vegetables. Interestingly enough, a number of dishes that are widely thought to be Israeli, such as falafel and hummus, in fact originated in Arab countries.

# JEWISH CUISINE

According to Claudia Roden in *The Book of Jewish Foods*, "every cuisine tells a story. Jewish food tells the story of an uprooted, migrating people and their vanished worlds. It lives in people's minds and has been kept alive because of what it evokes and represents. The Bible recalls in Exodus the wistful longings of the Jews for the foods they had left behind in Egypt."

Depending on whom you speak to, there are theories that there is no such thing as Israeli cuisine or Jewish food and that local regional food becomes Jewish when it travels with Jews to new homelands. What is familiar fare in one Jewish community may not even be known to the Jews of another region. Jews developed new recipes wherever they went by both adopting local customs and adapting local foods to their kosher diets. Frequently Jewish cooks would make a traditional recipe their own by using a special spice or a new ingredient.

Jewish life centered on tradition and holidays, especially the Sabbath. Special foods for important holidays and occasions were part and parcel of these traditions. For instance, during Passover, no leavening agents (flour and wheat) can be used, and some recipes were changed to accommodate this biblical restriction. Substitutes included ground almonds, potato flour, matzo meal, and matzos. In the Bible, laws for Sabbath (from Friday sunset to Saturday sundown) prohibit any work, including lighting fires and cooking. A different type of meal is prepared using dishes that slowly cook on a low heat from Friday night until lunch on Saturday, or by using cold salads and dishes that can be eaten cold, including a wide variety of dairy and vegetable dishes.

# ORIGINAL FOODS OF THE HOLY LAND

In biblical times, the ancient Hebrews were a nomadic desert people who had a number of indigenous plants available to them, the first being barley, which is probably the oldest grain. Fields of barley greeted the Jews when Joshua led them from their desert wanderings into the Promised Land. Later on, there came cracked wheat (or bulgur) and semolina, millet, and fava beans. Lentils were among the first plant cultivated and, of course, were mentioned in the Bible in the story of Esau and Jacob. Chickpeas probably arrived between A.D. 200 to 400. Couscous arrived in the fifteenth century. Other foods that were staples of the early

Jewish diet are still in use today. These included wine; bread; salt; peaches; honey; olives; fish; garlic; melon; olive oil; ethrog/citron; bitter herbs; lamb; dairy products made from milk such as butter, cheese, and sour milk; cucumbers; leeks; onions; wild garlic; grapes; figs (when Noah sent out the dove from the ark, it brought back a fig leaf); dates; game; goat; ducks; geese; fish; wine vinegar; walnuts; almonds; pistachios; and pomegranates.

From A.D. 200 to 400 cabbages, beets, celery, turnips, radishes, carobs, apricots,

*Pomegranates*

peaches, quinces and pears, apples, mulberries, mustard seeds, aniseed, mint, sage, marjoram, bay leaf, saffron, caraway, and coriander gradually became known to the Sephardic Jews. At the same time, conquering armies and their cooks brought a number of important spice trees—cinnamon, nutmeg, and cloves—which are not native to Israel but were planted there by these people. Such foreign peoples as the Romans introduced basil and oregano, while the Persians brought roses to make rose water, rose syrup, and rose petal jam.

Travelers, merchants, peddlers, rabbis, preachers, teachers, students, beggars, and pilgrims on their way to and from the Holy Land were vehicles of gastronomic knowledge as they carried news and descriptions of exotic dishes in far off lands. At times they even brought exotic ingredients with them. In this way, these travelers helped introduce and familiarize the Jewish communities with the foods and ingredients of other Jews around the known world.

By the seventh century, there were many traveling Jewish merchants, and for a while they were the only merchants in Europe and the Middle East. In their capacities as traders, importers, middlemen, and wholesalers, they served as an important source of exchange (of goods and information) between east and west. They also played an important role in Byzantine commerce, bringing eastern goods to Europe. The camel caravan trade was concentrated in their hands and their ships plied the Mediterranean Sea. As Marranos (converts who still practiced Judaism in secret), Jewish traders were among the earliest arrivals in South America along with the conquistadors. Because food items played a major part in their trade, it had an impact on their cooking. Their cuisine was shaped by their mobility as they moved from place to place during periods of migration and exile, caused by the destruction and dispersion of their communities and of the establishment of new ones.

Beginning with the destruction of the second Temple, these wandering Jews brought dishes from their old homelands to their new ones. While certain familiar ingredients were lost in the process, they were replaced by new ones, which resulted in many changes to established and cherished recipes. After 3000 years of moving and migration to almost all parts of the world, each recipe was like a chapter from a history book, a reminder of life in a particular geographic place. These recipes became a link with the past.

It was not uncommon for many Jewish communities to exist within a country. Consequently, Jewish cooking would vary from one city to another, resulting in many versions of the same dish! Within the Sephardic community, there were as many separate cuisines and cultures as there were geographic areas. For instance, the cooking of the Jews of northern Morocco comprised Spanish, Jewish, and Arabic traditions. Recipes included rice combined with meat or fish, and paprika (a Spanish mainstay). Arab contributions included couscous, fried pastries with phyllo dough, kebabs, and stews. The Jews of Northern Morocco used fewer spices than the Jews of southern Morocco, who had adopted more of the local Arab cooking styles. The latter included cinnamon, nutmeg, and turmeric for color and flavor. Tradition dictated offering sweets to visitors accompanied by the greeting "May you live in sweetness."

Such herbs and spices as garlic, coriander, parsley, cumin, salt, and pepper are an important component of Middle Eastern cook-

*Spice market*

ing because they give the food its character and personality. The hot/spicy foods of the Yemenites and Bedouins (like mouth-burning zhoug) are thought to contribute to good health. In addition to zhoug, a typical Middle Eastern meal might include shatta, tahina, and spice mixtures like hawyij, and hilbeh. Salads are eaten at virtually every meal (usually scooped up by pita bread, which is an essential staple that eliminates the need for a fork with many dishes). Salads are even served for breakfast in many Israeli homes, especially on a kibbutz. Soup is a mainstay of a Yemenite home, usually prepared in the morning and allowed to simmer throughout the day. The fiery spices used in soups and other dishes are said to help cleanse the body and neutralize the effects of meat fat. Another characteristic of Middle Eastern soups is the use of lentils, bulgur, pine nuts, coriander, and fresh herbs. These hearty soups are meals in themselves. In addition, there is a huge range of filled foods, called *memuleh*, which provides a combination of colors, textures, and tastes. Memuleh are made from vegetables and fruits with a variety of stuffings, including meats. Lamb is usually the meat of choice and is frequently used for special occasions. It can be baked, grilled, cooked on a spit, or stuffed. Israelis love shashlik, which is seasoned lamb grilled on a skewer over charcoal.

Photo: Dalia Carmel

# KASHRUT:
# WHAT IS KOSHER?

For many Jewish people, the kosher kitchen is the spiritual center of the home. Maintaining a kosher kitchen and eating only kosher food is one of the ways in which everyday actions become sanctified. *Kashrut* is the word commonly used to refer to the observation of the Jewish dietary laws. The word kosher literally means "fit" or "proper" and describes the types of food that the Torah (Law) declares fit to eat and the ways they can be prepared.

All Jewish cooking and food preparation is based on the observance of the dietary laws (of kashrut/kosher) revealed as commandments by God to Moses at Mt.Sinai, and later elaborated on in a universal Talmudic legal reference for the Jewish people. Laws of kashrut deal with what is permitted (or kosher) and what is forbidden. The interpretation of the kosher laws varies somewhat from country to country. The laws of kashrut apply only to the eating of animal products, since all plants-fruits, vegetables, nuts, herbs, spices, grains (everything that grows in the ground or on trees) are kosher. It is not difficult to keep kosher. All foods in the kosher kitchen are included in one of the three classifications: meat, dairy, or pareve.

For meats to be kosher, they must come from animals that both chew the cud (eat grass and leaves), have cloven hooves (so they cannot hold prey and be carnivores), and must be ritually slaughtered. The parts of the animal that can be used must be soaked in cold water and salted with kosher salt (to remove all the blood, since eating blood is forbidden) before cooking. The Bible says: "Thou must not eat flesh with its life blood in it... thou shalt not eat the blood for the soul resides in the blood." Animals must be slaughtered in the ritual manner called *shehitah*.

Meat that is allowed includes beef, lamb, veal, and goat. Pork is strictly forbidden. In America, the sciatic nerve, or the hindquarters where the nerve has not been removed is also forbidden (in remembrance of Jacob's struggle with a mysterious stranger/angel one night, injuring Jacob's thigh and leaving him with a limp). Unless a butcher takes the time to remove it, those cuts from the leg are banned (such as leg of lamb). In other countries, butchers may or may not remove this nerve, making the cuts kosher. Ritually slaughtered barnyard poultry are generally kosher. However, all birds of prey or carrion, and such other birds as owls, storks, and ostriches cannot be eaten.

There are not many laws governing the eating of fish, but to be kosher a fish must have both fins and scales, and shellfish are forbidden. Under the laws of kashrut, Jews cannot eat shark, eel, octopus, squid, reptiles, turtles, snails, frogs, or insects. Swordfish is considered kosher in some countries but not in the United States. Fish do not have to be ritually killed or soaked and salted to remove the blood. Tradition dictates that fish and meat may be eaten at the same time, but not served on the same plate!

Any food derived from milk is considered dairy, including all types of milk, butter, yogurt, and cheese. Dairy products must come from kosher animals and cannot be cooked or served with meat or poultry. If a food has even the smallest amount of dairy in it, that food is deemed to be dairy (today many processed food products have minute amounts of dairy in them, like certain instant oatmeals)

Tradition dictates that one must wait between eating a dairy and a meat product. If dairy is eaten first, there is no waiting period. However, if meat is eaten first, the waiting period can vary from one to five hours. In homes where Jews keep kosher, there are separate sets of dishes, pots and pans, and utensils for meat meals and dairy meals.

Pareve applies to foods that are neither meat nor dairy or derivatives of them, and these items can generally be served with either meat or dairy meals. Vegetables, fruits, and non-dairy product substitutes (such as oil-based margarine) are pareve. Other pareve foods include juices, noodles, grains, and eggs. Fish is also considered pareve.

# JEWISH HOLIDAYS

Jewish holidays seem to involve either feasting or fasting—nothing in between! All Jewish holidays begin at sundown because the Bible notes that when the world was created "there was evening and morning of the first day."

ROSH HASHANAH (New Year, or Head of the Year) marks the beginning of the Jewish High Holy Days and starts the Jewish year. Rosh Hashanah is celebrated with prayer, contemplation and soul searching. This is the time to evaluate actions and contemplate lifestyle changes. According to traditional Judaism, it is during this period that divine judgment on each person's life is made, when one's future is written for the coming year in the Book of Life (who shall live and who shall die). The end of Yom Kippur (see below) seals this "fate." It is also a time of joy and hope for the year to come, and during services the shofar, or ram's horn, is sounded as a reminder of spiritual awakening to arouse Jews from complacency and self satisfaction, and awaken them to reflection and action. In ancient days it served to call the people to prayer and announce the beginning of the holiday.

It is customary to dip apples in honey and eat sweet foods to symbolize the hope for a good sweet New Year, a year that will be blessed with good health, happiness, and fortune. Round loaves of challah are also eaten. They serve as a symbol of the cyclical and eternal nature of life and they express the hope that the coming year will be complete, unbroken by tragedy. The Sephardic Jews celebrate by serving traditional delicacies made with honey such as baklava, pinonate, and tishpishti.

Custom dictates that on the second day of Rosh Hashanah, a fruit not tasted since last season is eaten before dinner to celebrate the newness of the year and to thank God for another year. Bitter and sour foods are usually avoided during this holiday, as well as nuts (because the numerical value of the word "nut" in Hebrew has the same numerical value as the Hebrew word for "sin").

YOM KIPPUR (Day of Atonement) is the holiest day of the Jewish year and is sometimes referred to as the "Sabbath of Sabbaths." By partaking in fasting, prayer, and charity, we ask God for forgiveness for our sins against Him, and from people whom we have harmed or offended during the past year. We must seek that person's forgiveness before asking forgiveness from God. This is a concept that is unique to Judaism. The Talmud teaches that "the Day of Atonement forgives sins between man and man." Sins against God may be forgiven throughout the year, but this is the day that man has more access to God.

On the eve of the holiday, a simple meal is usually served. While many people prefer to eat bland foods, or foods that are not salty or spicy before fasting, others like to have a full stomach. If you drink a lot of coffee or soda, it is a good idea to taper off at least a week before fasting to avoid the withdrawal from caffeine! After a day of prayer, contemplation, and fasting for 25 hours, the "break the fast" meal is served at the end of Yom Kippur, marking the end of the High Holy Days. Breaking the fast also depends on individual tastes and traditions. Many people like to have a light, simple meal of bland foods with family, others prefer having a more lavish meal, breaking the fast with family and friends. Still others prefer to eat light, but want something filling, easy, and satisfying. Meals of dairy foods, lox and bagels, or kugels are popular. The meal is composed of dishes that can be completely prepared ahead, and that require only a quick reheating, since no one wants to wait longer than necessary to eat.

Rosh Hashanah, Yom Kippur, and the days in between are known as the 10 Days of Repentance or Return:

"On Rosh Hashanah the decree is signed and on Yom Kippur it is sealed... but Repentance, Prayer and Good Deeds can annul a harsh decree."—High Holiday Prayer Book

The 10 days of Repentance and Return are followed by The Season of Our Rejoicing: SUKKOT, the Feast/Festival of Booths. The Torah commandment to "rejoice" is mentioned more often in connection with this holiday than for any other. The Torah refers to Sukkot as

Chag Hasuccoth, the Festival of Booths or the Festival of the Tabernacles because we are commanded to dwell for seven days in tabernacles or booths. The word sukkot means "booth," and refers to the temporary shelters or huts (called tabernacles in the Bible) built when the Jews left Egypt and lived in the wilderness for 40 years before entering Israel. The holiday is celebrated in the synagogue and at home with family and friends, and centers around the sukkot—a temporary shelter (in one's yard) with temporary walls and evergreen branches, bamboo, or corn stalks for a roof that must be open to the sky. Many families decorate the walls and roof of the sukkot by hanging fruits and vegetables (or photos or drawings of them), or stringing berries and popcorn for hanging. All meals are supposed to be eaten in the sukkot. Casseroles, hearty soups, and items easily carried from kitchen to the sukkot are perfect for this holiday. Many people like to prepare recipes using fall fruits or vegetables.

Sukkot is also referred to as the Feast of Ingathering, because the holiday occurs during the time of the gathering of the harvest. Sukkot was one of the three pilgrimage festivals that took place during the time of the Temple in ancient Israel. Everyone was supposed to make the journey to Jerusalem and "appear" before God for this festival. Arriving two weeks after Rosh Hashanah, Sukkot lasts nine days. It is very similar to Thanksgiving since both give thanks for a bountiful harvest. It is felt that the idea for Thanksgiving came from this holiday.

The climax or final day of Sukkot ("season of our joy") is reached on SIMCHATH TORAH (simchath means "joy" or "great rejoicing"—the rejoicing with the Torah), marking the completion of the reading of the Five Books of Moses (Old Testament). In the synagogue the Torah is read on Mondays, Thursdays (which were market days in ancient times), and Saturdays. It takes a year to complete the reading aloud of the Torah, which is then rerolled and the reading starts all over again. All the Torah scrolls are brought out from the Ark where they are housed, and everyone sings and dances around the synagogue to thank God for giving us the Torah.

CHANUKAH (Festival of Lights), a happy holiday, is celebrated for eight days and commemorates a miracle that occurred over 2,000 years ago in the second century b.c., when the Jews under Mattathias and his son Judah Maccabee were victorious over their Greek oppressors in a fight for religious freedom. When the Temple was recaptured, the Jews wanted to rekindle the Menorah and to rededicate the Temple that had been spoiled by the enemy. Only a single small jar of pure oil that would burn for one day was found, since all the acceptably pure oil had been defiled. It would have taken eight days to prepare or acquire acceptably pure olive oil to burn. Tradition says that the small jar of oil burned for eight days—until the new oil was available. This miracle is the focus of the Chanukah celebration, and one candle is lit in a menorah each night for eight nights. To celebrate, blessings of thanksgiving are offered, money (Chanukah gelt, either real or chocolate), and/or gifts are exchanged, songs sung, and games played. The most popular game is spinning the dreidel (a special four-sided top with a letter on each side). Depending on which letter is up when the dreidel stops, money or candy is won or lost. This game originated because of an edict of the Romans forbidding the Jewish people to study the Torah. So they studied in secret, and if the Romans were sighted, they would hide the scrolls and gamble, playing with the dreidels.

Chanukah is replete with foods and desserts fried in or made with oil. Latkes (potato pancakes) with applesauce and sour cream are favored by Ashkenazic Jews, while Sephardic Jews serve *bimuelos*, which are round doughnuts rolled in cinnamon and honey. Israelis serve *sufganiyot* (jelly filled doughnuts—from the Greek word *surgan* meaning puffed and fried). Joan Nathan, in her book *The Jewish Holiday Baker*, mentions that the oil used for fried foods coincides to the end of the olive pressing at this time of year. "Greek women claim their loukomades—deep-fried puffs dipped in honey or sprinkled with powdered sugar—resemble the cakes the Maccabees ate." From Persia to Mexico, almost every culture has a fried dessert. A final note: Judah Maccabee never ate a *latke*, he never even saw a potato. Potatoes did not reach Europe until the Conquistadors brought them from

Peru and Ecuador in the sixteenth century and they did not come into use in Europe or the Middle East until 200 years later. By then the custom of eating foods cooked in oil on Chanukah had been long established!

*"And they shall sit every man under his vine and under his fig tree"*
—Micah 4:4

TU B'SHEVAT (the New Year of the Trees) is celebrated on the full moon or fifteenth day of the month of Shevat. The fifteenth in Hebrew letters is *tu* hence the holiday's name. It is a minor festival that has gained importance in the last decade as an environmental celebration. In Israel it is celebrated as Jewish Arbor Day and reminds us of the return to the land after wandering in the desert for 40 years. God instructed the Jews to revive the land and plant trees, fruits, vegetables, and grain. For the past 50 years or more, Jews from all over the world sent money for the planting of trees in Israel.

The holiday is usually celebrated by eating the fruit of trees and vines that grow in Israel: almonds, apples, apricots, figs, grapes, pistachios, walnuts, olives, and pomegranates. In the Bible (Leviticus 19:23-5), people are prohibited from eating the fruit of trees during the first three years after planting. This ensures that the trees will mature, bear fruit, and live a long life.

PURIM is a fun holiday and is celebrated with great merrymaking. Its beginnings lay in tragedy: a decree of death for the Jews. In the end, the Jews were not annihilated and their enemies were conquered. Purim commemorates the miracle that happened in Persia and is celebrated by the reading of the Book of Esther. The story tells how Queen Esther and her wise uncle Mordecai saved the Jewish people from being killed by the wicked Haman. Children (and some adults) love this holiday because they dress up in costumes, and are encouraged to make a lot of noise and shake noisemakers when Haman's name is mentioned during the reading of the story. It is a time for parties, feasting, and drinking. Foods are usually exchanged among friends, money is given to charity, and a festive holiday meal is enjoyed. *Hamantaschen* (three-cornered filled pastries supposed to resemble Haman's hat) are traditional for Ashkenazi Jews, while Sephardic Jews serve *foulares* (hard-cooked eggs in pastry supposed to represent Haman in jail or on the gallows). Purim is one of the three times during the year that it is traditional to serve *kreplach*; since kreplach have hidden stuffing, they are also served on Shavous and Yom Kippur. (God's answers are hidden and His presence in the Purim story is truly hidden). In fact, God's name is not mentioned in The Book of Esther at all.

PASSOVER (the great holiday of freedom) lasts for eight days. The holiday got its name because the Angel of Death passed over the homes of the Jews during the last plague when the first born of every Egyptian died. The Jews had placed lambs' blood on their doorposts to distinguish them from the Egyptians. It also celebrates the liberation and deliverance of the Jews from slavery more than 3000 years ago.

Every year at the seder (order of the service), the story is retold in the reading of the Haggadah, which precedes the dinner. During the holiday no leaven bread (only matzo and matzo products) is eaten, because in their haste to leave Egypt the Jews had no time for their bread to rise. One of the most important reasons for the seder and retelling of the story of the Exodus is that in every generation each Jew must see themselves as if they personally were taken out of Egypt, and hear of the many miracles God performed for their ancestors. The holiday begins with a thorough cleaning of the home, especially the kitchen, to remove every crumb of *hametz* (leavened food). Special plates and utensils are used during Passover that are not used during the rest of the year. Since all hametz is forbidden, Jews have created special recipes for observing the holiday. Ashkenazi cuisine and customs differs from that of the Sephardic Jews in that their meals feature gefilte fish, chicken soup with matzo balls, kugels, and tsimmis. The Sephardic Jews eat dishes made with rice, corn, beans, and peas during Passover. Ashkenazi do not.

INDEPENDENCE DAY or Yom Ha'atzma is celebrated in Israel. It is a time when all Israelis remember those who died in the struggle for an independent Israel. Israel was established in 1948. After the sun sets, there is dancing in the streets, singing, and fireworks. Picnicking is one way the national holiday is enjoyed.

LAG B'OMER is the fifty days that separate the going out of Egypt from the giving of the Torah (Shavuos). It also commemorates the end of an epidemic that wiped out a large number of Jewish scholars, and so became a day of rejoicing.

SHAVUOS heralds the celebration of the spring harvest and the giving of the Torah at Mt. Sinai, when the Jewish people became a real nation. Their identity was established with the acceptance of the Torah with the words "We will do and we will hear." This is a holiday where cheese and dairy are customarily eaten because the Torah is often compared with "milk and honey," and because the people were not yet well versed in the laws of kosher slaughtering so they refrained from eating meat. Traditionally blintzes, borscht (beet soup), and cheesecakes are eaten. It is also the festival of the fruits, celebrating the bringing of the first fruits to the Temple. In the synagogue the Book of Ruth is read. Three-sided kreplach filled with meat or cheese are traditionally eaten on Shavuos, since three is a prominent number in Jewish tradition (three patriarchs, three parts of the Bible).

TISH B'AV is observed as a day of mourning and fasting. In 586 B.C. in a war between the kingdom of Judah, Egypt, and Babylonia, the Babylonians won, the Temple was destroyed, and the Jews were taken into captivity. Seventy years later when the Persians defeated the Babylonians, the Jews returned to Israel, and rebuilt the Temple. In A.D. 70, 650 years later, the Romans under General Titus again destroyed Temple. Only the Western Wall of the courtyard was left standing, and the Jews were again taken into captivity. The Temple has never been rebuilt. Only the Western (Wailing) Wall remains. In addition, this day commemorates the departure of the Sephardic Jews from Spain in 1492.

In the past fish was traditionally served and meat and fowl were not eaten. The fast is broken with cheeses, eggs, and vegetables by the Sephardic and fish or lox with bagels by the Ashkenazic Jews.

SHABBOS (Sabbath) is the time when God rested from creation, and is a day when all thoughts of work are put aside. It is observed from sunset Friday night to sunset Saturday night. An atmosphere of tranquility and family unity descends upon the house. It is a day of rest—physically, mentally, and emotionally. It is a time to relax with family and friends. The commandment to observe Shabbos was one of the first given by God at Mt. Sinai. Shabbos is seen as a bride or queen and the woman of the house lights the Sabbath candles to welcome this holiday. A big family meal is usually served on Friday night.

In most of the world, Passover lasts for eight days, but among the Moroccan and Turkish Jews the holiday is extended and MIMOUNA festivities begin. Mimouna (or Mimuna, or Maimuna) is a celebration of liberty, community values, hospitality, friendship, and togetherness.

On Mimouna Eve, on their way home from services, Jews stop to visit the Rabbi's family, the Hazzan (the cantor), their parents, friends, and their neighbors, in that order. Turkish men throw coins, candy (symbols of the wealth and food the Jews brought with them when they left Egypt) and grass (a symbol of the reeds of the Red Sea) to children who eagerly await them.

Moroccans call this Maimuna and in every home, the rallying point of the celebration is the festive table that is decorated with flowers and stalks of wheat, and displays the symbolic holiday foods and an array of sweets. Among the decoration are symbols of good luck—a plate of fresh flour with a coin, a jar of honey, a bunch of fresh wheat, different greens, and fresh raw fish.

Traditionally this is the time of matchmaking for the young people of the community—a time for courting and looking for a future bride (or groom). After eating, everyone goes out in the streets and single people mingle under their parents' watchful eyes. The large Moroccan community in Israel holds Maimuna outside where a picnic-like atmosphere prevails with eating, drinking, and singing.

In some places, early the following morning, families in coastal cities get up and head for the seashore. They splash their faces with water, and step barefoot in the ocean—in memory of the miraculous crossing of the Red Sea (which took place historically on the last day of Passover) that ended in freedom. People who live inland go to the local wells, springs, rivers, or swimming holes. Afterward, there are picnics with lots of music, dances, and laughter.

It is difficult to determine this holiday's origin and there is a question of the meaning of Mimouna. Speculation includes these ideas: Mimouna comes from the name *Maimon*. Or Maimonides' father, (who had lived in Fes, where Mimouna is said to have originated) died on that day. Or it comes from the Hebrew/Aramaic word *mammon*, which means riches or prosperity. The underlying presumption is that an individual's productivity, the nation's bounty, and personal and national wealth are determined on Mimouna Day. And lastly, it contains the Hebrew word *emunah*, or "faith."

# TERMS USED IN THIS BOOK

**BAHARAT** is a combination of spices including cinnamon, cloves, nutmeg, cumin, coriander, pepper, and paprika. It is used mainly in Arabic countries.

**BROAD BEANS** (fava) can differ in color from beige to olive green to a purplish color. They are found in the cuisines of Egypt and Greece, Cyprus, Turkey, and Arabic countries and are also used dried.

**BULGUR** is the Turkish word for hulled wheat with a nut-like flavor.

**CARDAMOM** is a spice that has a sweet flavor and is available in seeds (in pods) or ground.

**CHICKPEAS** or garbanzo beans have been used since ancient times in Egypt and Greece. They are round, tan, and about the size of marbles. Dried chickpeas must be soaked before using.

**CORIANDER** and cilantro come from the same plant, which is a member of the parsley family. **CILANTRO**, the leaf, is either a love or hate taste. Ground coriander seeds are also used in cooking.

**CUMIN** is a spice native to Egypt and was used in ancient times. It is popular in Middle Eastern as well as Indian and southwestern American cooking.

**FENUGREEK** is a spice indigenous to the Eastern Mediterranean countries, and used mainly in Yemen cooking to make *hilbeh*. It is also an important ingredient in curry blends.

**FETA** is a white crumbly cheese, originating in Greece, made from goat's or ewe's milk.

**OKRA** is a green pod vegetable with a point at one end and is a native of Africa.

ORANGE FLOWER WATER is a fragrant liquid distilled from orange blossoms and used as a flavoring in dishes and especially desserts.

POMEGRANATE is a red fruit known since ancient times. It is a native of southwestern Asia. It is very popular in Persian cooking where it is used for its juice or made into syrup, while the edible seeds are used in dishes or as a garnish.

SAFFRON is the most expensive spice in the world since the stamens of thousands of crocuses are needed to produce a tiny amount. It is usually used to add color and fragrance to a dish.

SESAME SEEDS have also been used since ancient times in the Middle East. These tiny white seeds are used in making halvah and tahini.

SUMAC is the dried crushed red berry of the sumac tree. It has a lemony flavor that is both pleasant and sour to taste.

TAHINA is also called tahini in some countries, and is the oily paste made from toasted sesame seeds. Smooth and thick like peanut butter, it needs stirring before use since the oil tends to separate out. Depending on the brand used, taste can differ.

ZA'ATAR is a combination of thyme, marjoram, sumac, salt and sometimes sesame seeds that is used in many recipes or as a dip with bread and other condiments. It is from Syria and Lebanon.

# ❧ CONDIMENTS AND SPICES ☙

# ⊰ BAHARAT ⊱
## (MIDDLE EASTERN SPICE MIXTURE)
### Makes 2 1/2 cups

Baharat means "spice" in Arabic and is derived from the word *bahar* (pepper), so it is a mixture of spices with black pepper. Baharat can be bought at Middle Eastern groceries and markets. It is also quite easy to make fresh for yourself. Just keep it stored in an airtight spice jar. There are many different variations. This version is from Judith Amrani's family. You can either use ground spices from the store or buy whole spices and grind them at home (a coffee grinder works fine).

| | |
|---|---|
| 1/3 cup ground black pepper | 2 teaspoons cardamom, ground |
| 1/4 cup coriander powder | 1/4 cup ground nutmeg |
| scant 1/4 cup cinnamon | 1/2 cup paprika |
| scant 1/4 cup cloves, ground | 1/3 cup ground turmeric |
| 1/3 cup ground cumin | |

Mix all ingredients. Keep a small amount in a spice jar and freeze the rest in plastic baggies to keep it fresher.

# ⚜ HAWAYIJ OR HAWAJ ⚜

*Makes 5 tablespoons*

A traditional Yemenite spice mix, this is used in many types of recipes.

*6 teaspoons black peppercorns*
*3 teaspoons caraway seeds*
*1 teaspoon saffron threads*
*1 teaspoon cardamom seeds*
*2 teaspoons turmeric*

Using a mortar and pestle (or in a blender), pound (or combine) the peppercorns, caraway seeds, saffron, and cardamom together. Stir in the turmeric and place in a covered jar.

# ⊰ HILBEH ⊱

*Makes about 1/2 cup*

Hilbeh is used in southern Yemen, and hulba, a slightly different version is used in the north.

It is used for many purposes in cooking: on bread, vegetables, as a salad dressing, with meat or poultry. Fenugreek was virtually unknown in Israel until the Yemenite tribes brought it with them during their mass immigration when El Al planes brought them to "the promised land on the wings of eagles."

*2 teaspoons fenugreek seeds*

*2 garlic cloves*

*3/4 cup chopped cilantro leaves*

*1/2 teaspoon salt*

*2 teaspoons lemon juice*

*1 small hot chili, seeds removed, or a dash of chili pepper (optional)*

Soak the fenugreek seeds in 1/2 cup cold water overnight, or until a jellylike coating appears on the seeds.

Drain the water and place the seeds in the blender or processor with the garlic and cilantro. Blend until mixture is a coarse purée, then add the salt, lemon juice, and chili if you are using it. Add a small amount of cold water if needed to make sure mixture is well puréed.

Place in a covered jar or container and refrigerate until ready to use.

Sometimes the mixture is seasoned with zhoug (page 49).

# ⊰ HULBA ⊱

*Makes about 1/2 cup*

This is used as a fiery accompaniment to falafel or as a dip for bread.

1 cup boiling water

3 tablespoons fenugreek seeds, crushed to a fine powder

3 tomatoes, coarsely chopped

2 tablespoons finely chopped garlic

salt

3 whole cardamom pods, crushed or 1/8 teaspoon cardamom seeds

1 teaspoon caraway seeds

1/4 teaspoon ground coriander

1/2 teaspoon ground hot red pepper

Pour the boiling water over the crushed fenugreek seeds and let sit for 2 to 3 hours.

Purée the tomatoes in a food processor then push through a fine sieve (over a bowl). Drain the fenugreek in a fine sieve. Stir the fenugreek into the tomato purée.

With a mortar and pestle, mash the garlic and salt together to form a paste. Add the cardamom, caraway, coriander, and red pepper, mashing vigorously until a smooth mixture is formed. Add the spice mixture to the tomato mixture, mixing well.

Serve at once or store in a tightly covered container in the refrigerator.

# ⊰ SEVEN SPICE MIXTURE ⊱

*(not counting pepper!)*
*Makes about 1 cup*

This is similar to Baharat. It is often used to flavor meat dishes, stews, lamb, and some lentil soups.

6 tablespoons black peppercorns

3 tablespoons coriander seeds

3 tablespoons broken cinnamon sticks

3 tablespoons whole cloves

4 tablespoons cumin seeds

2 teaspoons cardamom seeds

2 whole nutmegs

6 tablespoons paprika

Grind everything but the nutmegs and paprika in a spice grinder. Grate the nutmegs and along with the paprika, add to the ground spices. Place in a jar with a tight lid and shake well to mix everything. Store mixture in a cool, dry place.

# ⊰ ZA'ATAR ⊱

*Makes about 1 cup*

Za'atar means "wild thyme" and is a Middle Eastern spice blend used in hundreds of recipes. Dip some bread or pita in olive oil and then in za'atar.

*1 cup dried thyme*
*1/4 cup toasted sesame seeds (optional)*
*1 tablespoon sumac*
*1/2 teaspoon salt*

Place the ingredients in a small jar, cover tightly, and shake well to mix. Store in a dry, cool place.

# ⊰ ZHOUG ⊱

*Makes about 2 cups*

There are as many recipes for this spicy condiment as there are ways to spell it! It is served with oriental Jewish dishes. More than a condiment, zhoug is believed to ward off disease and strengthen the heart! The number of chilies varies with the degree of "heat" you like!

| | |
|---|---|
| small green chili peppers | 1 teaspoon pepper |
| 1 1/4 cups chopped fresh parsley | 1 teaspoon salt |
| 1 cup chopped fresh cilantro | 1 teaspoon ground cumin |
| 2 tablespoons minced garlic | 2 tablespoons olive oil |

In a food processor or blender, purée enough chili peppers to make a cup. Remove from processor.

Purée the parsley and cilantro together and add the cup of chili peppers, blending well. Add the garlic, seasonings, and olive oil, blending well.

Place the mixture in a jar and refrigerate. It will keep for a few months.

# ⊰ PRESERVED LEMONS ⊱

*Makes 5 to 6 cups*

This is a Moroccan side dish, which is a tangy addition to salads, casseroles, and more.

*10 lemons*
*1 1/2 cups coarse sea salt*
*1/4 cup or more fresh lemon juice (optional)*

Cut 9 of the lemons in half and then each piece into thirds. Slice the remaining lemon into thin slices.

Place the salt in a large ceramic or glass bowl and add the lemon pieces. Press the salt into the lemons and gently squeeze the lemons so they release their juice.

Pack the lemons into a sterilized jar, and place the lemon slices around for decoration. Spoon in any remaining salt and pour in any lemon juice that is in the bowl. If necessary, add more lemon juice so the lemons are completely covered. Seal the jar and place in a cool dark place for two weeks before using.

The lemons will keep for up to six months. After opening, refrigerate the lemons.

# ⊰ TAHINA SAUCE ⊱

*Makes 1 cup*

Tahini is a paste made from sesame seeds and it is used in many recipes throughout the Middle East. When lemon juice and garlic are added, it becomes a salad served with pita bread for dipping. It is also used at meals to moisten and enrich the taste of almost every dish.

*1/2 cup tahini paste*
*1/4 cup fresh lemon juice*
*2 tablespoons chopped fresh parsley*
*1 teaspoon finely minced garlic*

Combine the tahini paste and 1/4 cup water, mashing with a fork.

Add the remaining ingredients one at a time, mixing well after each addition.

# ⊰ STRAINED YOGURT ⊱

*Makes about 3 cups*

*1 quart plain yogurt*

Line a fine sieve with two layers of cheesecloth and place over a large bowl. Pour the yogurt into the cheesecloth, bring the sides together and tie to make a "bag." Hang the bag over the bowl in a cool spot and let the yogurt drain for at least 3 hours. Do not do this in the refrigerator or the yogurt will set and not drain. Every now and then squeeze the bag with your fingers to remove as much liquid as possible.

When yogurt has drained for at least 3 hours, place in an airtight container and refrigerate. It will keep up to 5 days.

# ⵠ YOGURT CHEESE ⵠ

## LABANEH
### Makes about 1 1/2 cups

Labaneh is a sour cheese made from yogurt.

*1 recipe of strained yogurt
(page 52), not yet refrigerated*

*1 teaspoon fine grain salt
(optional)*

*extra-virgin olive oil (optional)*

*sprig of fresh rosemary
(optional)*

*ground pepper, mint, or paprika
(optional)*

When the yogurt has been strained for 3 hours or more, place the bag back in the sieve and open it. Stir in the salt if desired.

Cover the yogurt with the cheesecloth and place a heavy can or weighted plate on top. Let labaneh sit at room temperature for at least 2 hours.

Place in the refrigerator for another 2 hours. Then carefully wipe the sides and bottom of the cheesecloth with paper towel and leave the yogurt in the cheesecloth in the refrigerator in an airtight container for up to 4 days. If desired, after chilling the cheese can be rolled (by hand) to the size of golf balls and stored in a lidded jar with extra-virgin olive oil to cover, and a sprig of rosemary.

To serve, just spread on bread or crackers, or remove balls from the oil, drain well, and roll balls in ground pepper, mint, or paprika before spreading. Best when served with a little olive oil sprinkled on, freshly ground pepper, and small amounts of finely chopped herbs like parsley and oregano.

# ⊰ MEZZE ⊱
## (APPETIZERS, SNACKS, AND STARTERS)

# ⊰ CHEESE BALL WITH WALNUTS ⊱

*Serves 12*

1 pound feta cheese (with liquid squeezed out by pressing with a fork)

1 pound cream cheese

2 cups pitted kalamata olives

1 cup loosely packed fresh basil leaves

3 to 5 small garlic cloves

1 cup walnuts, coarsely chopped

1/2 to 1 cup extra-virgin olive oil

The day before serving, combine the feta and the cream cheese, mixing well. Place two layers of cheesecloth on a round strainer and place the cheese mixture on the cheesecloth. Place a large empty bowl under the strainer (to absorb the surplus liquid). Cover and place in the refrigerator for a whole day.

Before serving, place the olives on a serving plate. Shape the cheese mixture into a ball with a flat bottom and place the mixture of cheeses on top of the olives.

Place the basil in a food processor with the garlic and 1/2 cup walnuts. Slowly add the olive oil. Stop when the mixture begins to resemble a paste. Don't let it get too oily.

Pour basil mixture over the cheese ball. Spread remaining chopped walnuts on top of cheese.

# ⊰ CRESCENT OLIVE PUFFS ⊱

*Makes 3 to 4 dozen puffs*

These puffs can be made a day ahead, and reheated before serving.

*1 cup butter or margarine, at
room temperature*

*3 cups all-purpose flour*

*1 tablespoon baking powder*

*1/2 teaspoon salt*

*1 teaspoon paprika*

*4 ounces Gruyère or cheddar
cheese, grated*

*about 1/2 cup lowfat yogurt*

*6-ounce can pitted black olives or
green olives stuffed with
pimiento (or a combination),
well drained on paper towels*

*1 large egg mixed with 1 tea-
spoon water (egg wash)*

*1/4 cup sesame seeds (optional)*

Place the butter, flour, baking powder, salt, paprika, and cheese in a food processor and process until mixture becomes crumbly and just begins to bind together.

Add enough yogurt to combine with flour/cheese mixture and form a ball of dough. If the mixture is too dry, add more yogurt. If it is too sticky, add a little more flour.

Wrap the dough in plastic wrap and refrigerate for 30 minutes or more. Do not let it get so hard that you cannot roll it out.

Preheat oven to 375°F.

Divide dough into 2 or 3 balls.

On a lightly floured board roll one ball at a time until dough is about 1/4-inch thick. Cut out circles with a 2-inch round cookie cutter, and place one olive in the center of each circle.

Fold part of the dough over the olive, forming a crescent shape and pinch edges together. Continue until all the dough or olives are used.

Place crescents on a nonstick jelly roll pan and brush each crescent with the egg wash. Sprinkle sesame seeds on the crescents if desired, and bake 15 to 20 minutes or until golden brown.

# ⤞ EGGPLANT WITH TAHINI ⤝

## BABA GHANOUSH or BABA GHANNOOJ
### Makes about 2 cups

*B*aba is an Arabic word for father. According to Malvina Liebman in her book *Jewish Cookery*, "the name of the dish means 'indulged father,' said to derive from a doting son's preparation of it for his toothless father." This rich, creamy dip/salad is loved all around the Mediterranean and Israel.

| | |
|---|---|
| 1 eggplant (about a pound) | 1 tablespoon extra-virgin olive oil |
| 1/4 cup fresh lemon juice | |
| 2 tablespoons tahini paste (or more) | 2 tablespoons finely chopped onion (optional) |
| 1 to 2 garlic cloves, peeled and finely chopped | 1 tablespoon finely chopped flat leaf parsley |
| about 1 teaspoon salt | |

Preheat the oven to 375°F.

Lightly grease a baking sheet.

Halve the eggplant lengthwise, piercing the skin a few times with a fork, and arrange, cut sides down, on prepared baking sheet. Bake the eggplant in the middle of the oven until very soft, about 40 minutes.

Cool the eggplant until it can be handled, and scrape the flesh away from the skin. Place the eggplant in a food processor or blender. Add the lemon juice, tahini, garlic, and salt and process until smooth. Adjust to your taste by adding more salt, lemon juice, garlic, or tahini.

Pour into a serving bowl and sprinkle the top with the olive oil, onion if desired, and chopped parsley.

# ⊰ FAVA BEANS ⊱

*Serves 6*

When the fava beans are puréed (after cooking), mixed with a little olive oil and salt, and topped with a little za'atar they become *bye-sar*, a North African cousin of hummus. Pita is dipped in the byesar and then in a mixture of ground cumin, cayenne pepper, and salt.

*1 cup uncooked fava beans*

*2 to 3 garlic cloves, peeled (optional)*

*6 hard-cooked eggs, whole or peeled and chopped*

*3/4 cup tahini sauce*

*6 tablespoons extra-virgin olive oil*

*1 1/2 tablespoons chopped fresh parsley*

*pita bread*

*chopped onions (optional)*

In a large pot, soak the fava beans overnight with water to cover.

Drain the water and place the beans and garlic (if using) back in the pot and cover with fresh water.

Bring the water to a boil, reduce heat, and cook the beans until they are very soft, about 1 hour. If needed, add more water to the pot.

Drain the beans when done (they will crumble in your hands). Divide the beans into 6 portions and place in bowls. For each portion sprinkle on top of the beans 1 chopped hard cooked egg, 2 tablespoons tahini sauce, a tablespoon of olive oil, and some parsley.

Serve with pita bread and chopped onions, if desired.

# ⊰ FISH ROE SALAD/SPREAD ⊱
## TARAMOSALTA
### Serves 10 to 12

It can be confusing at times to understand that what we use as a dip
or spread, other cultures call a salad. This is a wonderful Greek dip
or spread, and is similar to a pâté. The basic ingredient is made from
the roe of carp called *tarama*. Versions vary from place to place and
cook to cook, varying in the taste, texture, and ingredients.

*10-ounce jar tarama*

*1/4 to 1/3 cup minced onion*

*2 to 3 cloves peeled garlic
(optional)*

*3 to 4 cups fresh white bread
crumbs (from any roll or dense
bread with crusts removed)*

*or 1 1/2 cups mashed potatoes
plus 1 1/2 cups bread crumbs*

*juice of 1 1/2 lemons, or more*

*1/2 cup extra-virgin olive oil, or
more*

*finely chopped flat leaf parsley*

*olives*

Place the tarama into a bowl, and cover it with cold water. Let
tarama sit for half an hour. Place two layers of cheesecloth in a
sieve and pour in the tarama. Using the cheesecloth to help
squeeze, remove as much of the water as possible.

Place the drained tarama, onion, garlic (if using), and 3 cups of
bread crumbs in a food processor or blender. While processing,
slowly add the juice of 1 lemon and the olive oil in a slow
steady stream, processing until taramosalata is light in color
and smooth with a medium-thick consistency. If the taramosalata is too thin, add additional bread crumbs. If it is too thick,
add a little cold water. Taste, and decide if you want to add the
remaining lemon juice or more olive oil.

Sprinkle with chopped parsley and serve with olives, pita
bread, and raw vegetables.

# ⊰ HUMMUS ⊱

*Makes 3 cups*

Use as a dip, or a spread for sandwiches. If you want a really thick hummus, do not use the saved liquid.

15-ounce can chickpeas
  (garbanzo beans), drained and
  liquid saved

1 cup tahini sauce

1/2 cup fresh lemon juice

1 to 2 garlic cloves

1/2 to 1 teaspoon cumin

1/2 teaspoon salt

1/4 teaspoon paprika

3 to 4 tablespoons extra-virgin
  olive oil

2 tablespoons chopped parsley,
  for garnish

pita bread for dipping

Purée the chickpeas, tahini, lemon juice, garlic, cumin, salt, paprika, and 1 teaspoon olive oil in a blender or food processor. If needed, use the saved liquid from the chickpeas to thin the hummus.

To serve, scoop the hummus on a serving plate, and with the back of a spoon, make a depression around the top. Fill with the remaining olive oil. Garnish with chopped parsley, and dip with pieces of pita bread.

Photo: Sheilah Kaufman

# ⚜ TOMATO SPREAD ⚜

## SHAKSHOUKA
### Makes 3 to 4 cups

A spicy Sephardic and Israeli dish—no Middle Eastern menu is complete without it. Most cooks have their own personal version of this favorite. This dish can be used as an appetizer or dip. This is the Perez family recipe, and Leah usually makes a lot of shakshouka in the summer when she buys tomatoes and green peppers in bulk at the outdoor market.

| | |
|---|---|
| 4 tablespoons olive oil | salt |
| 2 onions, chopped | freshly ground pepper |
| 4 garlic cloves, chopped | 1 teaspoon ground cumin |
| 4 tomatoes, coarsely chopped | pinch of cayenne or chili powder |
| 2 large green peppers, chopped | 1 or 2 large eggs per person |
| 1 chicken bouillon cube | (optional) |
| 3 ounces tomato paste | |

In a large skillet heat the oil and sauté the onion until soft and translucent. Add garlic, cook for a minute, stirring, and add the tomatoes and peppers. Cover the skillet and steam for about 10 minutes.

Add 1 cup water, bouillon, tomato paste, and spices. Cover and cook for 20 to 30 minutes, stirring occasionally.

If desired, break whole eggs and slide them gently onto the sauce—try not to break the yolks! Cover and cook until eggs are firm.

Serve 1 or 2 eggs per person with sauce (and plenty of good bread or pita to wipe up the sauce!).

Refrigerate to store.

# ⚜ STUFFED GRAPE LEAVES ⚜

*DOLMATHES, SARMIS*
*Makes about 3 dozen*

These are as elegant as ladyfingers, and therefore shaped that way!

9-ounce jar grape leaves in brine

1 large onion, finely chopped

1/2 cup extra-virgin olive oil

1 cup uncooked long-grain
   white rice

1/4 cup minced parsley

1 tablespoon chopped fresh dill

1/2 tablespoon chopped
   fresh mint

salt

freshly ground pepper

1/4 cup pine nuts

2 1/2 cups beef or chicken broth,
   or part white wine

lettuce (optional)

6 tablespoons lemon juice

lemon wedges, for garnish

Remove the grape leaves from the jar, rinse them well with boiling or hot water, or let soak in the water for a few minutes to remove the brine. Drain the leaves and soak them in cold water for a few minutes. Drain again, cut off the stems, and dry with paper towels.

In a large skillet, sauté the onion in 1/4 cup of the olive oil until soft and golden. Add the rice, parsley, dill, mint, salt and pepper to taste, pine nuts, and 1 cup of the stock. Bring to a boil. Lower the heat and simmer, covered, until all liquid is absorbed—about 10 minutes. Let mixture cool slightly. Taste and adjust seasonings if needed.

To assemble dolmathes, place a leaf, shiny side down, on a flat surface. Place approximately one teaspoon of the mixture in the center of the leaf. Fold over the sides like an envelope and roll up the leaf. Be careful not to roll it too tightly, as the rice expands during the final cooking time. Continue this procedure until all the leaves and filling are used up.

Line a deep, large pan with a few of the torn leaves or some lettuce leaves, or use cheesecloth to prevent the dolmathes from sticking to the bottom of the pan. Sprinkle the leaves with the lemon juice and the remaining 1/4 cup olive oil. Pour the remaining 1 1/2 cups broth and 1 cup water carefully down the sides of the pan. Weigh down the grape leaves with a large heatproof plate to prevent the rolls from opening up during the final cooking.

Cover the pan, and simmer on low for about 35 minutes or until the rice is tender. Let the rolls cool in the pan. Remove them to a serving platter with a slotted spoon and refrigerate until well chilled.

Just before serving, sprinkle some olive oil over the dolmathes to make them shiny.

Garnish with lemon wedges.

NOTE: These do not freeze well, but they will keep in the refrigerator for several days.

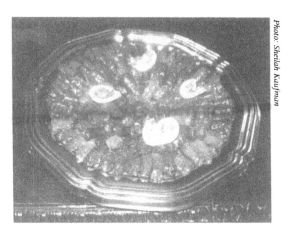

# ⊰ WALNUT DIP ⊱

*Makes about 2 cups*

Leah Spiegel contributed the recipe for this delicious dip. She is originally from Israel and is now a well-known caterer in New Jersey.

*2 cups chopped walnuts*

*1 medium head garlic, peeled*

*2 slices of sourdough bread or white bread with crusts removed, or two 2-ounce whole wheat pitas*

*juice of 1 lemon*

*about 1/2 cup extra-virgin olive oil*

*salt*

*freshly ground pepper*

Combine the nuts, garlic, and bread in a food processor, chopping until mixture is fine. Pour in the lemon juice, and chop another few seconds. Slowly pour in the olive oil while the processor is running, and continue processing until a paste is formed. Add salt and pepper to taste and mix well. Place in a covered container and refrigerate.

Dip will keep for a week or two in the refrigerator. Use on bread, crackers, veggies, or with fish or chicken.

# ⚐YOGURT AND CUCUMBER SPREAD/SALAD ⚑

*TZATZIKI or TSATSIKI*

*Serves 6 to 8*

Versions of this dish are popular from Northern India, through Greece, the Balkans, and in Israel. Needless to say, there are many variations of this salad. Perfect as part of a mezze assortment, it can double as a side dish, or as a topping for vegetables or fish. In Turkey a variation is called *cacik*.

| | |
|---|---|
| *1 large English cucumber, peeled, seeded, and sliced in half lengthwise* | *1 tablespoon fresh lemon juice* |
| *1/2 to 1 tablespoon sea salt* | *freshly ground pepper, preferably white* |
| *1 1/4 cups strained yogurt (page 52)* | *2 to 4 large garlic cloves, minced* |
| *2 tablespoons extra-virgin olive oil* | *1/4 cup fresh mint leaves* |
| | *2 tablespoons chopped fresh parsley (optional)* |

Cut the cucumber into julienne pieces (matchstick size) or dice, then sprinkle with salt and place in a large colander and let it sit for an hour (to drain).

In a large bowl combine the yogurt, olive oil, lemon juice, pepper, and garlic. Mix well, cover and refrigerate until serving.

Before serving, using a wooden spoon, beat the yogurt sauce until smooth. Cut or tear the mint into small pieces. Dry the cucumber pieces by squeezing them in paper towel to remove all of the water. Stir the pieces of cucumber into the yogurt mixture, and add the mint (and parsley if using) and mix well to combine.

Add salt and pepper to taste, mix well, and serve with pita bread, crackers, vegetables, etc.

# ❧ SOUPS ❧

*Sephardic Israeli Cuisine*

# ⊰ COLD YOGURT SOUP ⊱

## LABAN
### *Serves 4 to 6*

2 tablespoons oil

3/4 cup finely chopped onion

3 to 4 garlic cloves, finely
  chopped

7 ounces fresh (baby) spinach,
  washed, dried, and torn into
  large pieces

1/2 cup rice

salt

freshly ground pepper

2 cups plain yogurt

1 tablespoon chopped fresh mint
  or 2 teaspoons dried mint

1 cucumber, peeled and chopped

1 teaspoon dried dill (optional)

In a small skillet, heat the oil and sauté the onions and 2 cloves of the garlic until soft. Stir in the spinach and cook, stirring until it wilts. Then add the rice, 3/4 cup water, and salt and pepper to taste. Mix well, cover, and cook over low heat for about 20 minutes, or until rice is done.

Remove skillet from the heat, place the mixture in a bowl and refrigerate until chilled.

In a large bowl combine yogurt, remaining 1 to 2 cloves garlic, mint, cucumber, salt to taste, and dill if using. Stir in chilled spinach mixture, and serve cold.

# CUCUMBER WITH YOGURT SOUP

## TARATOR
### Serves 4 to 6

Viviane's father fled Sofia, Bulgaria in 1944 and went to Tehran. There (and in Bulgaria), this recipe is called *tarator*. Her mother, who was born in Russia, also found refuge in Iran and calls this recipe *akrochka*. The Persian name of the dish is *mast o khiar* and is made slightly differently.

2 to 3 small cucumbers, peeled and diced

1/2 cup golden raisins, washed and drained (to plump them)

3 cups plain yogurt

small amount of sour cream (optional)

2 scallions, whites with a little green, chopped

2 to 3 garlic cloves, crushed or minced

2 to 3 tablespoons coarsely chopped walnuts

1 tablespoon chopped fresh dill

1 tablespoon chopped fresh mint

salt

freshly ground pepper

In a large bowl, combine all the ingredients and season to taste with salt and pepper. Cover and refrigerate until serving.

# ⊰ EGYPTIAN GREEN
HERB SOUP ⊱

*Serves 4 to 6*

*M*elokhia, a member of the mallow family, grows wild in the spring-
time in the Middle East. Spinach or chard can be substituted. You
can buy frozen *melokhia* in Middle Eastern supermarkets.

*1 quart homemade chicken broth
or canned broth*
*1 or 2 packages (14 ounces each)
frozen melokhia*
*salt*
*freshly ground pepper*
*1 tablespoon tomato paste*

*4 to 6 garlic cloves*
*1 tablespoon butter*
*2 teaspoons ground cilantro*
*2 tablespoons fresh lemon juice*
*1 large onion, peeled and chopped*
*1 to 2 tablespoons white vinegar*

Place the broth in a large pot and add the melokhia. Bring to a
boil and let it boil for 2 to 3 minutes. Stir in salt and pepper to
taste, mixing well.

Reduce heat to simmer, add the tomato paste and simmer for 20
minutes, stirring occasionally. Soup should be thick and smooth
and the melokhia dissolved.

Finely chop the garlic and mash into a smooth paste in a mortar
and pestle. In a small skillet, melt the butter and sauté the
cilantro and garlic, stirring for a minute or two.

Add the garlic mixture to the soup, stir, and simmer for another
3 minutes. Stir the lemon juice into the soup, taste, and adjust
seasoning.

Combine the chopped onion and enough vinegar to cover in a
small bowl and set aside.

Ladle the soup into bowls and serve with the onions in vinegar.

This soup is sometimes served on top of dried pita bread covered with white rice and poached chicken *(melokhia fatta)*.

# ⊰ FAVA BEAN SOUP ⊱

*Serves 6*

This soup is only made by Sephardic Moroccans and served for Passover because that is what the Hebrews ate in Egypt. According to the Bible, broad beans were one of the foods the Jews missed after their exodus from Egypt. They were and still are a basic staple in Egypt since the time of the Pharaohs.

*1 pound skinless split dried broad beans or frozen fava beans, defrosted and peeled*

*4 cups chicken broth or water*

*salt*

*2 tablespoons olive oil*

*6 garlic cloves, finely chopped*

*1 teaspoon paprika*

*2 teaspoons cumin*

*1/2 teaspoon turmeric*

*pinch of cayenne (optional)*

*juice of 2 lemons*

*bunch of fresh cilantro, washed and chopped*

Soak the beans in water for a couple of hours, then drain well.

Place the chicken stock or water in a large pot, add the beans and bring to a boil. Remove any scum, cover, reduce heat to simmer, and cook for 2 hours, or until the beans are soft and fall apart.

Add salt to taste, remove the beans and mash with a potato masher, or place in a blender or food processor with a little of the cooking liquid and purée. Return the beans to the pot and cooking liquid.

In a small skillet, heat the oil, add the garlic, and sauté until golden. Add the paprika, cumin, turmeric, and cayenne if using. Mix well and add to the soup. Simmer, covered, another 20 to 30 minutes. If soup is too thick add a little more broth or water.

Just before serving, stir in the lemon juice and cilantro and mix well.

# ⊰ HARIRA ⊱

*Serves 8 to 10*

This is Morocco's most famous soup, and is used to break the fast during the holy month of Ramadan.

| | |
|---|---|
| *1 cup chickpeas (dried or canned)* | *1 teaspoon ground cumin* |
| *2 pounds cubed beef* | *1 tablespoon ground coriander* |
| *2 or 3 small beef bones* | *1 teaspoon cinnamon* |
| *1 cup dried lentils* | *freshly ground pepper* |
| *3 tablespoons olive oil (or more)* | *1/2 cup all-purpose flour* |
| *3 medium onions, diced* | *1 cup orzo pasta* |
| *1/2 bunch celery, diced* | *salt* |
| *3 or 4 fresh tomatoes, seeded and chopped* | *1 bunch fresh parsley, chopped* |
| *1 teaspoon turmeric* | *1 bunch fresh cilantro, chopped* |
| *pinch of saffron* | *1/2 cup fresh lemon juice* |
| *1 teaspoon ground ginger* | |

If the chickpeas are dried, soak them overnight, rinsing well. If canned, rinse well several times before using. Place 1 1/4 gallons water in a large pot and add the meat, bones, lentils, and chickpeas.

In a skillet heat the oil and sauté the onions and celery, stirring, and cook until both are bright and translucent.

Add the tomatoes, cook and stir for another few minutes, mixing well then add the mixture to the soup. Add the turmeric, saffron, ginger, cumin, coriander, cinnamon, and pepper, mixing well. Cover and cook on low heat for 1 1/2 to 2 hours.

In a small bowl whisk together the flour and 1 cup water, then whisk into the soup. Add the orzo, salt, chopped parsley, and cilantro, mixing well. Cook covered for another 30 minutes and stir in the lemon juice. Continue cooking soup, uncovered, for another 15 minutes while stirring from time to time. Soup should be thick at this point. If soup is too thick, you may add more water to dilute it.

# ⊰ LEMON CHICKEN SOUP ⊱
## AVGOLEMONO
### Serves 6

This soup can be found from Greece to Egypt. The Jewish community in Greece dates from the time of the first dispersion. While in Greece, the Jews adopted this soup. When many Greek Jews went to Israel after 1948, they introduced this soup. Mimi Sheraton, in her book *The Whole World Loves Chicken Soup*, points out that cloves are sometimes added in Greece, a bay leaf in Albania and Turkey, cinnamon in Lebanon and Tunisia, and cumin or cardamom in Egypt.

*6 cups chicken broth or stock\**

*2 stalks celery with leaves*

*1 /2 onion, cut into chunks*

*1 / 2 cup uncooked white rice*

*2 cups finely chopped cooked chicken breast (optional)*

*1/4 teaspoon ground cardamom (or your favorite spice) (optional)*

*3 large egg yolks*

*3 tablespoons fresh lemon juice*

*salt*

*freshly ground pepper*

Heat the broth, celery, onion, rice, chicken (if using), and cardamom in a large nonreactive pot. Partly cover the pot and cook over low heat for about 35 minutes or until the rice is tender. Remove soup from the heat and remove any celery leaves, onion, and any whole spices.

In a small bowl beat the egg yolks and lemon juice gently with a whisk. Slowly whisk in a few spoonfuls of the hot but not simmering soup, beating constantly with the whisk. After 2 cups of the soup have been whisked in, slowly and carefully whisk the egg mixture back into the soup pot, beating constantly with the whisk. Do not let soup boil!

Season to taste with salt, pepper, and additional lemon juice if desired.

*If using canned broth or stock, refrigerate overnight, then remove all the fat from the top.

# ⚔ RED LENTIL SOUP ⚓

*Serves 6*

2 tablespoons vegetable oil

1 onion, chopped

2 large garlic cloves, finely
chopped

2 carrots, peeled and sliced thin

1 1/2 cups split red lentils,
cleaned and washed

2 1/2 cups vegetable stock or
beef or chicken broth

3 teaspoons salt

1 teaspoon coriander seed

freshly ground pepper

1 tablespoon flour

1 to 1 1/2 teaspoons cumin

crushed red pepper (optional)

juice of 1 lemon

Heat the oil in a large pot and sauté the onion and garlic, stirring, until onion is soft and translucent. Add the carrots and stir another 5 minutes. Add the lentils, vegetable stock, and 3 1/2 cups water and bring to a boil.

Mash together the salt and coriander seeds using a mortar and pestle.

Reduce heat to simmer, and stir in the mashed salt and coriander seeds. Stir in freshly ground pepper to taste. Cover and simmer for 30 to 60 minutes, stirring occasionally

Before serving, whisk together the flour and 2 tablespoons cold water in a small bowl and whisk into the soup, stirring until thickened slightly. Add cumin and crushed red pepper to taste if using, mixing well. Pour lemon juice on top just before serving.

# ⚜ TAMAR'S YEMINITE CHICKEN SOUP ⚜

*Serves 8*

Tamar Horn's parents left Yemen in 1937 on a British passport and moved to the Holy Land. Her father chose the city of Rehovot to live in since his married sister lived there. He supported his family, which included 11 children, by making mattresses, pillows, and blankets.

4-pound whole chicken, cut up

2 onions, peeled

4 to 6 carrots, peeled

bunch of leeks, whites only—
save the green tops

3 tablespoons fresh chopped
parsley

2 potatoes, peeled and cut into
chunks

1 butternut squash, peeled and
cut into chunks about
2 x 1-inches

2 chicken bouillon cubes

spices to taste including:

2 to 2 1/2 teaspoons hawaj

1 teaspoon ground cumin

turmeric (not needed if using
hawaj)

1 bunch fresh cilantro, washed
with stems removed

salt

freshly ground pepper

Place chicken in a large pot and add enough cold water to cover plus an inch more. Bring to a boil, and as chicken cooks, skim off scum. Reduce heat to medium, add onion, carrots, leeks, and parsley, cover and cook for 20 minutes then add potatoes and squash.

Stir in bouillon cubes and spices. Lower heat to simmer, cover, and cook until chicken is done, about 45 minutes.

Add cilantro and chopped greens from the leeks, and cook another 10 minutes. Remove chicken from pot, let soup cool and strain the broth.

Keep chicken separate. Tear or cut into pieces and add to soup before serving. If needed, add salt and freshly ground pepper to taste.

This soup may be made ahead or frozen.

*Sephardic Israeli Cuisine*

# ⇥ SALADS ⇤

*Sephardic Israeli Cuisine*

# ⁂ CARROT AND ORANGE SALAD ⁂

*Serves 4*

*1 tablespoon orange juice*
*1 teaspoon cinnamon*
*1 tablespoon sugar*
*pinch of salt*
*2 to 3 tablespoons lemon juice*
*1 teaspoon orange flower water*
*1 or 2 navel oranges, peeled and sectioned*
*1 pound large carrots, peeled and grated*
*lettuce leaves (optional)*

Combine the orange juice, cinnamon, sugar, salt, lemon juice, and orange flower water and mix thoroughly.

Place the oranges in a serving bowl. Sprinkle the grated carrot over the orange segments. Pour the sauce over the carrots and oranges, mixing well. Cover and chill until serving.

Before serving, you may want to drain off some of the juice. Place each serving on an individual lettuce leaf if desired, and serve.

# ⤐ DOREEN'S FATTOUSH SALAD ⤏

*Serves 4*

Leah Perez learned this from her step-mom Doreen who makes it for
their famous Sunday barbecues. It is sometimes referred to as
bread salad, or wet bread.

*2 pita breads (large size)*
*salt*
*freshly ground pepper*
*1/4 cup fresh lemon juice*
*1/3 cup extra-virgin olive oil*
*1 1/2 teaspoons sumac*
*1/2 head romaine lettuce, torn*
  *into bite-size pieces*

*1/2 cup coarsely chopped parsley*
*4 scallions, sliced, whites only*
*1/2 cup chopped or torn fresh*
  *mint*
*2 cucumbers, peeled and chopped*
*2 tomatoes, chopped*
*1 green pepper, diced (optional)*

Preheat oven to 375°F.

Place pitas on a cookie sheet and bake until golden and crisp
(about 15 minutes). Let bread cool then break into 1/2-inch
pieces.

Prepare dressing by mixing salt, pepper, lemon juice, olive oil,
and 1 teaspoon of the sumac in a small bowl.

In a large bowl, toss lettuce, parsley, scallions, mint, cucumbers,
and tomatoes (and green pepper if using).

Sprinkle remaining 1/2 teaspoon sumac over salad and add
toasted pita pieces. Pour dressing over salad and toss well.

Serve immediately.

# ⁂ JERUSALEM TAHINI SALAD ⁂

*Serves 6*

*3 large tomatoes, coarsely chopped*
*3 pickling cucumbers, coarsely chopped*
*1 bunch scallions, whites with a little green, coarsely chopped*
*1 bunch fresh parsley, coarsely chopped*
*1 bunch green mint, coarsely chopped*
*1 medium romaine lettuce, torn into bite-size pieces*
*salt*
*freshly ground pepper*
*1/2 cup extra-virgin olive oil*
*1 cup tahini*
*juice of 3 lemons*

In a large bowl, combine the tomatoes, cucumbers, scallions, parsley, mint, and lettuce. Add the salt, pepper, and oil, mixing well.

In a separate bowl, mix the tahini with a small amount of water to thin it. Gradually stir in the lemon juice. Add the tahini mixture to the vegetables and mix well.

If desired, a little more olive oil can be sprinkled on top of the salad.

# ⊰ TABOULEH ⊱

*Serves 8*

A unique Middle Eastern salad.

*1 cup cracked wheat (precooked bulgur wheat)*
*2 large tomatoes, diced*
*1/2 to 3/4 cup chopped scallions, whites with a little green*
*1/4 cup olive oil*
*1/3 to 1/2 cup fresh lemon juice*
*3/4 cup chopped fresh parsley*
*1 teaspoon salt*
*freshly ground pepper*
*1/4 cup chopped fresh mint leaves*

A few hours, or the day before serving, place the wheat in a large bowl and cover it with boiling water. Let it stand for 15 minutes, until the wheat feels tender, but slightly crunchy. Drain off the water and wash the wheat under the faucet 2 or 3 more times, then drain the wheat thoroughly.

In a salad bowl, combine the wheat, tomatoes, and scallions. Add the oil, lemon juice, parsley, salt, and pepper to taste. Stir and mix well, then garnish the salad with the mint leaves.

Cover the bowl and refrigerate for at least 2 hours before serving.

*Sephardic Israeli Cuisine*

# ❧ CHICKEN ❧

# ⚜ CHICKEN PIE ⚜

### BISTEEYA
*Serves 10 easily*

In many books, this is referred to as Pigeon Pie. This recipe is time consuming, but the end product makes for exceptional eating and is well worth the praise and delight that will come from your guests. It is usually eaten with the right hand directly from the serving dish.

*4 pounds chicken parts, with fat removed*

*1 to 2 large onions, finely chopped*

*1 cup chopped fresh parsley*

*1/4 to 1/2 cup chopped fresh cilantro*

*pinch of saffron*

*1/2 teaspoon ground turmeric*

*freshly ground pepper*

*salt*

*3/4 teaspoon ground ginger*

*2 cinnamon sticks*

*1 to 1 1/4 cups margarine*

*1/4 cup vegetable oil*

*1 pound blanched whole almonds*

*2/3 cup granulated sugar*

*1 teaspoon ground cinnamon*

*1/4 cup lemon juice*

*10 to 12 large eggs, well beaten*

*1/2 pound phyllo dough, defrosted and at room temperature*

*confectioners' sugar*

Place the chicken parts in a large pot with the onion, parsley, cilantro, saffron, turmeric, pepper and salt to taste, ginger, cinnamon sticks, and 1/2 cup of the margarine. Add 4 to 8 cups of water (being sure all the chicken pieces are covered), bring to a boil, then lower heat to simmer, cover, and cook for about an hour or until chicken is done.

Remove chicken from the pot, saving cooking stock but discarding the skin, bones, and cinnamon sticks. When chicken has cooled, tear the meat into bite-size pieces.

In a large skillet, heat the oil and brown the almonds lightly, then drain almonds on paper towels. Place the nuts in the food processor and chop fine.

In a small bowl combine the granulated sugar and the cinnamon, mixing well. Mix the ground almonds with the sugar and cinnamon mixture and set aside.

Bring the chicken stock to a boil and cook, uncovered, over high heat until it is reduced to about 1 3/4 to 2 cups of stock. Stir in the lemon juice and reduce heat to simmer. Pour in the well-beaten eggs, stirring rapidly and constantly until they cook and congeal. (They will resemble dry scrambled eggs and there should be no liquid remaining.)

The dish can be prepared a day ahead up to this point.

Preheat the oven to 425°F.

Grease the bottom and sides of a 9 by 13-inch glass pan or a 12-inch round baking pan.

In a small skillet, melt the remaining 1/2 to 3/4 cups margarine, pouring off any milky solids.

Place a sheet of phyllo on the bottom of the pan, or overlap several sheets on the bottom of the pan, and brush with melted margarine. Sprinkle with a little of the nut mixture, then place another sheet of phyllo on top, brush with melted margarine, and sprinkle with a little of the nut mixture. Repeat this step until you have used 4 or 5 sheets of phyllo.

Place the chicken pieces on the top sheet of phyllo and cover it with the congealed eggs. Place a sheet of phyllo on top of the egg/chicken mixture, brush it melted margarine and sprinkle with the nut mixture. Top with another sheet of phyllo, brush with melted margarine, and sprinkle with the nut mixture. Repeat this until you have used 5 sheets of phyllo.

If using a round baking pan, try and tuck the overlap of the last two sheets of phyllo neatly under the pie so it is completely enclosed. Brush the top of the pie with melted margarine and bake for about 20 minutes.

Shake the pan to loosen the pie and run a metal spatula around the edges, then tilt the pan and pour off any excess margarine. If possible, and depending on the pan used, invert the pie onto a nonstick jelly roll pan or a greased 14-inch round pizza pan. Brush the top of the pie with melted margarine and return to the oven for another 10 minutes or until top is golden brown, then tilt to removed any excess margarine.

Sprinkle top with confectioners' sugar, sprinkle very lightly with cinnamon and serve at once.

# ☙ CHICKEN BREASTS WITH KUMQUATS ☙
## TARNEGOLET BEMITYZ HADARIM
### Serves 4

Kumquats are originally from China, and are sometimes referred to as "Chinese oranges."

2 whole chicken breasts, boned
    and skinned, cut in long strips

all-purpose flour

salt

freshly ground pepper

3 tablespoons margarine

juice of 2 oranges

juice of 1 lemon

5 tablespoons honey

few dashes of Tabasco or
    favorite hot sauce

6 to 8 fresh kumquats, sliced (if
    not available use preserved
    kumquats [in a jar])

Toss chicken strips in flour mixed with a little salt and pepper and shake off the excess.

In a large skillet, melt the margarine and sauté the chicken just until it starts to firm up and is done. Remove the chicken from pan, place on a plate, and keep warm.

Add the orange juice, lemon juice, honey, Tabasco, and kumquats to the pan. Reduce heat to low and simmer the ingredients for a few minutes, stirring. When the mixture is reduced to a sauce consistency, return the chicken to the pan, and stir well to coat each piece with sauce.

Serve with rice.

NOTE: If a variation is desired, fresh kumquats can be sliced in half and added to a caramelized sugar syrup (half sugar/half water) to cook for a few minutes. A little Triple Sec can be added for flavor.

# ⚜ CHICKEN HAMIN ⚜

*Serves 8*

2 to 3 tablespoons extra-virgin
  olive oil
2 large onions, peeled and sliced
10 small potatoes, peeled
3 carrots, peeled
1 cup mixed lentils
1 chicken, cleaned and cut into
  serving pieces

salt
freshly ground pepper
3 tablespoons chopped fresh
  cilantro
4 to 6 dates
2 tablespoons sugar

Preheat oven to 225°F.

Place the oil in the bottom of a large pot, then add the onions, potatoes, carrots, lentils, chicken, salt and pepper to taste, cilantro, and dates.

Heat the sugar in another heavy pan until dark brown and caramelized and pour over the ingredients in the casserole. Add 6 cups water, or enough water to cover and bring to a boil over high heat.

Remove from heat, cover, and place casserole in the oven and bake for about 12 hours. After 6 hours of cooking, taste for seasonings and add more salt and pepper if desired.

# ⊰ CHICKEN WITH OKRA ⊱

## POLLO CON BAMYA

### Serves 4

The name of this recipe indicates the ethnic influences of Sephardic Jewish cuisine, but *bamya* is the Turkish word for okra, which Bulgarian Jews embraced. In 1346, Bulgarian King Ivan Alexander left his wife and married the Jewess Sarah, who became queen under the name of Theodora. In spite of her conversion to Christianity, she extended royal protection to her Jewish subjects. This led to a growing Jewish influence in the Bulgarian kingdom. This story has a striking similarity to the Story of Esther in which a Jewish woman married the Persian King Ahasuerus and helped to save her fellow Jews from extermination. This recipe is courtesy of Linda Forristal, from her book *Bulgarian Rhapsody*.

4 to 6 pounds chicken parts, or 4 whole chicken breasts

2 pounds okra

3 tablespoons white vinegar

4 medium tomatoes

2 tablespoons olive oil

1 medium onion, finely chopped

1/3 cup red wine

salt

freshly ground pepper

pinch of sugar

Wash the chicken and cut into desired portions and set aside.

Clean the okra by removing the stems, and place the okra in a medium bowl.

Mix the 2 cups water and the vinegar together. Pour the mixture over the okra and let the okra soak for 30 minutes.

Rinse the tomatoes under hot water, then peel them, remove their seeds, and chop.

In a 4- to 6-quart pot, heat the oil and fry the chicken and onion until brown. Add the chopped tomatoes, 3/4 cup water, wine, salt and pepper to taste, and sugar. Cover and cook over medium heat for 20 to 25 minutes (larger pieces will take longer).

Drain and rinse the okra, add it to the chicken and continue cooking until the chicken is done, about another 30 minutes. Taste and adjust seasoning.

Serve hot.

# ⚜CHICKEN WITH OLIVES⚜

*Serves 4 to 6*

2 pounds cracked green olives,
    pitted
1/4 cup olive oil
5 garlic cloves
2 ripe tomatoes, diced
2 to 2 1/2 pounds chicken
    breasts, split in half, skinned
    and boned

1/2 teaspoon turmeric
freshly ground pepper
pinch of saffron
1/4 cup chopped fresh cilantro
1/2 cup lemon juice

Place the olives in a small pot of cold water and boil for a minute. Pour out the water, replace with more cold water and boil for a minute, repeat again.

In a large skillet, heat the oil and sauté garlic and tomatoes. Add the chicken and spices and cook for 5 to 10 minutes, turning once. Drain the olives and add to the chicken with 1 cup of water. Cover and cook over low heat for 20 to 25 minutes, or until chicken is done.

Remove the cover the last 5 or 10 minutes and stir in the cilantro and lemon juice. Cook, stirring for another minute.

Serve hot.

*Sephardic Israeli Cuisine*

# ⊰ CIRCASSIAN CHICKEN ⊱

## CERKES RAVUGU
### Serves 6

A delicious alternative to chicken salad.

3 chicken breasts, boned and
  skinned

3 cups chicken broth or stock

3 slices day-old white bread,
  with crusts removed

2 tablespoons extra-virgin olive
  oil or walnut oil

1 tablespoon margarine

1/2 cup finely chopped onions

1 garlic clove, minced

1 teaspoon paprika

1/2 teaspoon salt

freshly ground pepper

1 1/2 cups walnuts (plus additional for garnish)

dash of hot sauce (optional)

1/4 cup chopped fresh parsley for
  garnish

Place the chicken breasts in a large pot with the chicken broth, bring to a boil, cover, and reduce heat to simmer. Cook gently for 15 to 20 minutes or until chicken breasts are done. Be careful not to overcook them. Remove chicken from the pot and save the cooking liquid. Let chicken cool, then cut chicken into strips, or shred.

Quickly soak the bread in some of the cooking liquid and squeeze the liquid out immediately. Crumble the bread and set aside.

In a small skillet, heat the olive oil and the margarine and sauté the onions for just a minute or two. Do not let the onions brown. Stir in the garlic, paprika, salt and pepper to taste, and remove the skillet from the heat.

Place the walnuts in the food processor and coarsely chop. Then add 1 cup of the reserved chicken broth, the onion mixture, and bread. Process for just a minute until mixed. Add salt and pepper to taste and a dash of hot sauce if desired and blend to make a smooth sauce. If sauce is too thick add a little more of the chicken broth.

Place the cooked chicken on a serving platter and pour the sauce on top. Mix well and garnish with paprika, parsley, and walnuts, if desired.

Serve cold or at room temperature.

# GRANDMA'S CHICKEN MEATBALLS

## KTZITZOT
### Makes 36 to 48 meatballs

I wanted to interview the cookbook author Zion Levi for this book, so I called information in New York. After getting the number, I called and explained to Mr. Levi that I was writing a cookbook and would like to use one of his recipes. He said that he did not know what I was talking about, and we finally realized I had the wrong Zion Levi. He did, however, tell me to call Ha Pisgah, a Middle Eastern restaurant in Queens. I called and "met" a lovely lady named Shelly Shalom (born in Jerusalem) whose parents were from Morocco. After talking for a while Shelly offered to share her Grandma Rachel Shalom's (from Tunis) recipe.

3 baking potatoes, peeled and cut into quarters

5 whole chicken breasts, boned and skinned

2 medium onions, grated

4 garlic cloves, finely chopped

1/2 cup chopped fresh parsley

1/2 cup chopped fresh cilantro or more if desired

2 pieces unsweetened challah, crusts removed

salt

freshly ground pepper

1 teaspoon paprika

1 tablespoon onion soup powder

dash of hot sauce, hot paprika, or cumin (optional)

2 large eggs, separated

vegetable oil for frying

about 3 cups tomato sauce (optional)

Boil the potatoes in water just until tender, then cool.

Grind the chicken in a food processor and place the ground chicken in a large bowl. Add the grated onion and garlic, mixing well. Grate the potatoes into the chicken mixture. Mix well and stir in the parsley and cilantro.

Run water over the challah, and squeeze to remove the water, then crumble the challah into the chicken mixture. Stir in the salt and pepper to taste, paprika, onion soup powder, and hot sauce if desired. Add the egg yolks, mixing well to combine all the ingredients.

Whisk or beat the egg whites until stiff and place in a small bowl. Shape the chicken mixture into golf ball-size balls and dip each into the egg whites.

In a large frying pan, heat the oil and fry the chicken balls on all sides until brown. Drain well. At this point you have 3 options: 1) pour your favorite tomato sauce over the chicken meatballs and bake at 350°F, covered, for 15 minutes, then uncover them and cook a little longer so the sauce gets thicker (if desired). 2) In another skillet place the chicken meatballs in your favorite tomato sauce and simmer on low heat for about 10 minutes. 3) Serve along with your favorite tomato sauce or with no sauce at all.

These chicken meatballs taste even better when reheated the next day.

# ⊰ MEDITERRANEAN CHICKEN ⊱
*Serves 8*

This dish is sweet, salty, pungent, and delicious. The prunes and olives make a sensational flavor combination. This is a perfect recipe for company, and can be easily doubled or even tripled. It tastes even better the next day.

MARINADE:

1 cup pitted prunes

1/2 cup chopped green olives

4 bay leaves

8 large garlic cloves, minced

3 tablespoons dried oregano

1/2 cup red wine vinegar

1/2 cup extra-virgin olive oil

juice of 1 lime

10 to 14 pieces chicken
(1 to 2 per person)

FOR BAKING:

1 cup white wine (something fairly sweet)

1/2 cup chopped fresh parsley or cilantro

Mix ingredients for the marinade. Place chicken in a nonreactive bowl or plastic storage bag, and add the marinade. Refrigerate covered (if using bowl), overnight.

Preheat oven to 350°F.

Place the chicken in a single layer, skin side up, in a shallow roasting pan. Pour marinade on top and pour the wine around it. Bake about 1 hour, basting from time to time.

Sprinkle with parsley or cilantro before serving. Pass pan juices separately.

Freezes and reheats well.

# ❧ FISH ❧

*Sephardic Israeli Cuisine*

# DAVID DAHAN'S MOROCCAN FISH WITH ANCHO CHILIES

*Serves 4*

Make this recipe as mild or spicy as you like by adjusting the chilies.

2 pounds rockfish, sea bass, snapper, or tilapia, filleted

salt

6 cilantro leaves with stems, torn into pieces

3 to 4 ancho chilies, sweet, mild, or spicy, sliced

1 cup coarsely chopped fresh cilantro

1/2 cup olive oil

5 garlic cloves, minced

1/2 teaspoon turmeric

1/2 teaspoon paprika, sweet or hot

freshly ground pepper

Sprinkle fish with salt to taste.

In a large skillet, place 3 of the torn cilantro leaves. Place the fish on top of the torn cilantro and place the remaining 3 torn cilantro leaves on top of the fish. Spread the ancho chilies and chopped cilantro around the fish.

Make a paste (using a mortar and pestle or food processor) with the oil, garlic, turmeric, and paprika. Pour mixture over fish. Sprinkle with freshly ground pepper.

Pour 1 cup water around the fish and cook on low heat, uncovered, until it flakes easily with a fork. If needed, add more water.

# ⊰ FISH STUFFED WITH DATES ⊱

*Serves 2 to 4*

4 pounds whole trout,
  red snapper, or white fish

salt

freshly ground pepper

1/2 cup chopped pitted dates

2/3 cup cooked rice

1/2 cup chopped pine nuts
  (or almonds or walnuts)

1 teaspoon powdered ginger

cinnamon

1 onion, sliced

1/4 cup white wine (optional)

Preheat oven to 350°F.

Clean the fish and season lightly with salt and pepper.

In a small bowl combine dates, rice, nuts, and ginger and stuff into the fish.

Skewer fish shut and rub fish skin with cinnamon and additional ginger.

Lightly grease a baking pan and top with onion slices. Place stuffed fish on the bed of onions and pour wine around it, if desired. Bake until fish flakes easily with a fork. Remove stuffing from fish and place on a serving platter.

Serve at once.

# ⚜ GRILLED FISH WITH CHERMOULA ⚗

*Serves 2 to 4*

Chermoula or charmoula is a spicy Moroccan fish marinade that will enhance the flavor of any fish, cooked in any way. This is another easy recipe with many versions, some of which include chopped onion.

*1/2 teaspoon saffron threads*

*4 tablespoons chopped fresh cilantro*

*3 tablespoons chopped fresh parsley*

*2 to 3 garlic cloves, finely minced*

*1 to 2 teaspoons paprika*

*1 1/2 teaspoons ground cumin*

*dash of cayenne pepper (optional)*

*3 tablespoons fresh lemon juice*

*6 tablespoons extra-virgin olive oil*

*salt*

*2 pounds whole fish or fish fillets*

Steep the saffron in 2 tablespoons of warm water, then drain.

Combine all the ingredients except fish in a large bowl and whisk together to blend.

Place the fish in a glass-baking pan and cover with the marinade. Cover the pan and let the fish marinate for at least 3 to 6 hours or overnight if possible in the refrigerator. Turn fish over a few times to ensure all parts have been in the marinade.

To cook, just grill or broil until fish flakes easily with a fork.

# ⚜ LEAH PEREZ'S MEDITERREAN FISH BAKE ⚜

*Serves 4*

4 teaspoons olive oil
1 small green pepper, chopped
1 garlic clove, minced
1/2 teaspoon cinnamon
1/2 teaspoon paprika
1/2 teaspoon turmeric
1/4 teaspoon cumin
hot pepper flakes (optional)

salt
freshly ground pepper
19-ounce can tomatoes with liquid
2 strips fresh orange rind
15-ounce can chickpeas, drained
1 pound firm white fish fillets

Preheat oven to 425°F.

In a skillet, heat 2 teaspoons of the oil over medium to high heat. Add green pepper and garlic, and sauté for 1 minute. Stir in spices, and salt and pepper to taste, and cook for another minute. Add tomatoes, breaking them up into chunks and simmer about 5 minutes until mixture is slightly reduced. Add the orange rind.

Place tomato mixture in an 11 by 7-inch baking dish. Stir in chickpeas, mixing well.

Arrange fish in single layer on top of tomato mixture. If the ends are thin, tuck them under. Drizzle the fish with the remaining 2 teaspoons olive oil and sprinkle lightly with salt and pepper.

Bake for 20 minutes or until fish flakes easily with a fork.

*Sephardic Israeli Cuisine*

# LYDIA WOLF'S FISH WITH TOMATO SAUCE AND PEPPERS

*Serves 4*

3 tablespoons olive oil

5 to 10 (or more) garlic cloves, chopped or minced

1 or 2 green bell peppers, sliced thin with seeds and ribs removed

1 red bell pepper, sliced thin with seeds and ribs removed

1 green chili pepper, sliced in strips with seeds removed (optional)

28-ounce can crushed or diced tomatoes

1 tablespoon paprika

crushed red pepper flakes (to taste)

1/2 teaspoon turmeric

salt

freshly ground pepper

2 pounds firm white fish, like sea bass, cut in fillets or steaks

1/4 cup chopped fresh parsley

In a large skillet over medium heat, heat the olive oil and sauté the garlic and peppers. Cook until soft, about 5 minutes. Add the tomatoes, paprika, red pepper flakes, turmeric, and salt and pepper to taste. Stir well to mix, then lower heat to simmer and cook, stirring for 5 minutes.

Lay the fish in the sauce in a single layer, spooning some sauce over the fish. Cover and simmer for 13 to 15 minutes, spooning additional sauce over fish a few times during the cooking. If desired, remove lid during the last 5 minutes to thicken the sauce. Then sprinkle with chopped parsley and serve immediately.

# ⪦ SPICY FISH ⪧

## HRAIME
### Serves 2 to 4

This is a Libyan version of spicy fish, which was often served as an appetizer before a holiday or before a Shabbat meal.

*3 tablespoons vegetable oil*

*juice of 1 lemon*

*2 tablespoons tomato paste*

*salt*

*5 garlic cloves, chopped fine*

*1 teaspoon ground cumin seed*

*2 to 3 teaspoons hot red chili, seeded, ribbed, and chopped (optional)*

*1 pound red snapper, sea bass, halibut or similar fish filets*

*lemon wedges for garnish*

In a large skillet, heat the oil on low heat.

Mix together 1/2 cup water and the lemon juice, tomato paste, salt to taste, garlic, cumin, and chili if using. Add to the skillet and simmer over low heat for 10 minutes.

Add the fish and 1 cup of water. Cover and continue to cook over low heat for 15 minutes or until fish is done.

Serve with lemon wedges.

Photo: Vivienne Roumani-Denn

*Sephardic Israeli Cuisine*

# ⚜ WALNUT STUFFED FISH ⚜

*Serves 2 to 4*

The Almog Tradex Company had a contest for the best recipe using nuts. This was one of the winning recipes.

| | |
|---|---|
| 1 fish, about 2 1/2 pounds | 1 chopped onion |
| salt | 1 head garlic (10 to 15 cloves), minced |
| 1 cup tahini sauce | |
| 1/2 cup fresh lemon juice | 2 tablespoons finely chopped fresh cilantro |
| 1 cup chopped walnuts | |
| freshly ground pepper | 1 tablespoon chopped jalapeño pepper (optional) |
| 1/2 cup extra-virgin olive oil | |

Preheat oven to 350°F.

Wash the fish well and pat it dry with paper towels. Rub the fish with salt and set aside for half an hour.

Combine the tahini and 2 cups water, mixing well, then stir in the lemon juice. Keep mixing until you get a smooth sauce. Add the chopped walnuts, salt, and freshly ground pepper to taste to the sauce.

In a small skillet, heat the oil and sauté the onion, garlic, cilantro, and jalapeño. Cook for 3 to 4 minutes, stirring. Add the onion mixture to the tahini sauce and mix well.

Place the fish in a lightly greased baking pan and stuff with most of the onion mixture. Place any remaining mixture on top of fish and cover with foil.

Bake until fish flakes easily with a fork.

# ❧ MEAT ☙

*Sephardic Israeli Cuisine*

# ᔥ BEANS WITH MEAT AND SPINACH ᔥ

## LUBYA B' SELK

### Serves 6 to 8

As a child, Vivienne called this the "green" beans (*lubya hedra*) to differentiate it from a similar dish made with a tomato base. Since it is like a stew, it is usually served with couscous or bread.

*2 tablespoons extra-virgin olive oil*

*2 bunches fresh spinach, leaves only, washed and drained well*

*1 bunch fresh cilantro, cleaned and chopped*

*6 green onions, green part only, chopped*

*1 head of garlic, peeled and chopped*

*1 teaspoon turmeric*

*freshly ground pepper*

*salt*

*1 pound of meat per person cut in 1-inch chunks*

*8 tablespoons navy or white pinto beans, washed and drained*

In a 4 to 6 quart pot, heat the oil and sauté the spinach. Cool, drain, and grind in a food processor. Return the spinach to the pot and add the cilantro, onions, garlic, turmeric, pepper and salt to taste, meat, and the beans.

Add enough water to cover all the ingredients and bring to a boil. Cover and let simmer for 2 hours, or until the beans are tender. If desired, remove the lid for the last 30 minutes of cooking.

*Photo: Vivienne Roumani-Denn*

# ⊰ COUSCOUS TAGINE ⊱

*Serves 6 to 8*

Gilda Angel points out in her *Sephardic Holiday Cooking* that under Roman domination, North Africa became the granary of the entire Roman Empire. Most of what was grown was exported, especially the grains, and the local population was left without sufficient food. The North Africans made use of semolina wheat middlings, a byproduct of flour milling, and a new food was born—couscous. Originally, the grains had to be moistened and rolled in one's hands, then dried and steamed (in the top part of a couscousière while the flavorful stew cooked in the bottom) until light and fluffy. Don't let the lengthy list of ingredients scare you away from this fabulous dish.

TAGINE:

- 1/2 cup extra-virgin olive oil
- 1 1/2 pounds boneless lamb, cut into large chunks or cubes (or chicken or beef; lamb is traditional)
- 3 cinnamon sticks
- 10 peppercorns, lightly crushed
- 1 teaspoon ground cumin
- pinch of saffron
- 10 whole cloves
- 1/4 teaspoon salt
- 1/2 pound dried apricots
- 1/2 pound raisins
- 4 ripe tomatoes, peeled and cut into wedges
- 2 large onions, peeled and cut into wedges
- 4 carrots, thickly sliced
- 3 celery ribs, cut into large pieces

- 16-ounce can chickpeas (garbanzo beans), drained
- 17-ounce can sweet potatoes, drained
- 2 large zucchini, sliced
- 6 artichoke hearts (canned or jarred), drained
- 4 to 8 cups chicken broth (or more)
- 17-ounce box couscous
- vegetable oil

HARISSA SAUCE:

- 2 tablespoons cayenne pepper
- 1 teaspoon fennel seeds
- 1 teaspoon caraway seeds
- 1 teaspoon ground cumin
- 2 garlic cloves, crushed
- 1/2 teaspoon salt
- 1 cup olive oil

GARNISH:

*1/4 pound dried currants*

*1/4 pound chopped almonds or*
  *pine nuts*

*1 pound dried prunes, soaked in*
  *white wine or water (optional)*


Preheat oven to 350°F.

Prepare the tagine: Heat the olive oil in a large skillet and cook the meat until the outside is browned. Place the meat in a large ovenproof casserole. Add the spices, apricots, raisins, and tomatoes. Bake, covered, for 45 minutes, or until meat is tender.

Add the vegetables to the casserole along with enough chicken broth to cover the entire mixture and bake for another 20 to 30 minutes.

Meanwhile, cook the couscous according to package directions. Remove from heat but keep warm.

To prepare the harissa sauce, grind together the spices, garlic, and salt with a mortar and pestle (or food processor). This mixture can be prepared ahead and kept in a tightly covered glass jar in the refrigerator until needed.

A few minutes before serving, add the olive oil to the spice mixture, place in a small pan, and cook, stirring constantly for 5 minutes.

Before serving the tagine, remove and discard the cinnamon sticks and cloves. Garnish with the currants and nuts, and prunes if desired.

Serve the tagine, couscous, and sauce separately. Let your guests mix the three together as they choose.

# ⚜ DANIELA SCIAKY'S SPINACH-WRAPPED MEATBALLS ⚜

*Makes about 24 meatballs*

1 pound fresh spinach leaves, washed

1 pound ground turkey

1/2 pound lean ground beef

1 large egg

1/4 cup chopped fresh flat leaf parsley

salt

freshly ground pepper

any spices, to taste

1 1/2 tablespoons matzo meal

1/4 cup fresh lemon juice

1/4 cup olive oil

3 lemons, sliced

Preheat oven to 350°F.

Place washed spinach leaves in a steamer basket in a large pot with 1/2 inch boiling water. Cover and cook for 2 minutes or until the spinach wilts. Rinse with cold water and drain.

In a large bowl combine meats, egg, parsley, spices, and matzo meal, mixing well. Roll the meat mixture into walnut-size balls and wrap a spinach leaf around each ball completely covering it. You may have to use more than one leaf or part of a leaf. Place the wrapped meatballs in a 9 by 13-inch glass baking pan. Cover meatballs with any remaining spinach leaves.

Combine 1/2 cup water, the lemon juice, and olive oil and pour over spinach and meatballs.

Cover pan tightly with aluminum foil and bake for 30 minutes.

Turn meatballs over, and check the liquid. Add more water, if necessary. Cook another 30 minutes or until meatballs are done.

Serve with lots of fresh lemon slices.

# ⊰ LAMB PIES ⊱

## LAHN BI AJEEN

These are sometimes called Lebanese pizzas. Ground meat and vegetables are often combined in Sephardic recipes.

DOUGH:

1 1/2 teaspoons dry yeast

1/2 teaspoon sugar

2 cups all-purpose flour

1/2 teaspoon salt

1/4 cup butter, melted and cooled

FILLING:

1 tablespoon extra-virgin olive oil

1 cup finely chopped onion

1 pound lean ground lamb

1/4 cup finely chopped parsley

1 teaspoon dried mint

1 tablespoon lemon juice

2 teaspoons tomato paste

1 cup pine nuts

1/4 teaspoon allspice

1/4 teaspoon cinnamon

salt

freshly ground pepper

1/2 teaspoon cayenne pepper (optional)

2 medium tomatoes, seeded and chopped

In a small bowl, combine the yeast, sugar, and 1/2 cup warm water. Stir and let sit for about 10 minutes until it begins to get foamy.

Place the flour and salt in a food processor. When the yeast is ready and the butter cooled, begin processing, adding the yeast first and then the butter. Continue to process for about 45 seconds more. Place dough in a lightly greased bowl, rub a little oil on top, cover with a towel, and let it rise in a warm place until doubled—about 1 hour.

In a large skillet, heat the oil and sauté the onions until soft. Stir in the lamb and cook, until almost no pink shows. Add the remaining ingredients, stirring to mix well. Taste and adjust seasoning if needed, then drain well.

Preheat oven to 425°F. Grease 2 baking sheets.

When the dough has risen, divide it into 12 pieces for lunch or dinner-size portions, 24 pieces for appetizer size. Roll each piece into a ball, flatten it with the palm of your hand, and stretch or roll into a circle about 6 inches in diameter (3 inches for appetizer size) on a lightly floured surface. As each round is finished, place it on a baking sheet.

Spread each round generously with a few tablespoons of filling, spreading all the way to the edges, since the meat will shrink towards the center while baking. Bake for 8 to 13 minutes, depending on whether you want to fold them and eat them with your fingers or have them with a crisp rim like a pizza disk.

Serve immediately or cool on a wire rack. Reheat 2 to 3 minutes in a 350°F oven just before serving. If they are frozen, heat for 5 minutes.

# ⊰ MAFRUM ⊱

*Serves 6 to 8*

This dish from Libya has no English name equivalent, my friend Vivienne told me. Her family is from Benghazi, Libya. She left when she was 12 with her family. Her mother was progressive and didn't push her daughter to cook while at home. She felt that there would be time enough to learn when Vivienne had her own home. People in the know just call this dish Mafrum. It is an appetizer or a side dish to couscous and is served on every special occasion including holidays and Friday night Shabbat dinners.

STUFFING:

1 pound ground beef

1 onion, grated

1 tablespoon freshly chopped parsley

4 garlic cloves, finely chopped

salt

freshly ground pepper

1/8 teaspoon ground cinnamon

1 teaspoon turmeric (optional)

POTATOES:

5 medium potatoes, peeled (or large canned artichoke hearts or eggplants)

2 teaspoons salt

flour for dredging

2 large eggs, beaten

vegetable oil for frying

BASE:

2 large tomatoes, sliced

1 medium onion, sliced thin

potato slices

1 tablespoon tomato paste

Combine the stuffing ingredients and set aside.

Slice each potato (or artichoke heart or eggplant) lengthwise, leaving every 2 slices connected on one side and separated for every other set of 2 slices. Each potato yields about 2 to 3 "sandwiches." Use any potatoes that do not cut nicely into slices for the base. Sprinkle all slices inside and out with salt and let stand for 5 minutes. Rinse well and dry on a towel.

Stuff the inside of each potato "sandwich" with about 1/4 cup of the stuffing. Cup it in the palm of your hand to tighten it gently. Repeat with remaining ingredients. Roll each mafrum in the flour and then in the beaten eggs.

Heat the oil in a pot or deep fryer and fry the stuffed potatoes over medium heat for 5 minutes or until both sides are lightly brown.

Place the tomato slices on the bottom of another lightly oiled pan. Cover with the onion slices and any potatoes that did not make sandwiches.

Mix the tomato paste in 2 cups of water and add to the pan. Bring to a boil, reduce heat, and place the fried stuffed potatoes on top. Simmer, covered for 20 minutes.

Serve warm.

*Photo: Vivienne Roumani-Denn*

# ⊰ MEATBALLS IN DOUGH ⊱
*BAKED KIBBETH or KIBBI or KUBA*
*Serves 6*

This is the national dish of Lebanon. It basically is a mixture of ground meat (a combination of lamb and beef—one used to make the dough, the other to make the filling). These two simple ingredients have given birth to a vast variety of dishes, which are extremely nourishing and can be baked, stuffed, used with sauces, or added to any soup. The recipes for these "hidden meat" balls differs slightly from country to country. Reheating just improves the flavor. The easiest way to prepare kibbeth is to layer and bake it instead of making the dough, shaping the meatballs, stuffing the dough with a meat mixture, and frying them. This is a layered version. The lamb and beef are interchangeable.

DOUGH:

- 3/4 cup bulgur wheat
- 1 cup very finely minced onion
- 1 pound lean lamb (with a little fat), finely minced or ground twice
- 1 red pepper, seeded and ground/finely chopped, or chili pepper (optional)
- 1 teaspoon salt
- freshly ground pepper
- 1/2 teaspoon ground cinnamon

FILLING:

- 2 tablespoons plus 2 teaspoons olive oil
- 1/2 cup coarsely chopped walnuts or pine nuts
- 2 medium onions, minced
- 8 ounces ground lean lamb (or beef)
- 1/2 teaspoon cinnamon
- 1/4 teaspoon allspice
- salt
- freshly ground pepper

Prepare the dough: Soak the bulgur in 2 cups hot water for 30 minutes. It should double in bulk. Drain well and shake in a fine strainer or squeeze to remove all the water.

Combine the onion, lamb, red pepper, salt and pepper to taste, and cinnamon and set aside.

Combine bulgur with the uncooked ground lamb mixture (or chop it in the food processor for 15 to 20 seconds). If desired add an occasional tablespoon of ice water to keep the mixture smooth and cold. For the best results, refrigerate in a covered container for a few hours then knead again with your hands for a few minutes before cooking.

Preheat oven to 350°F.

Prepare the filling: In a small skillet, heat 2 teaspoons of the oil and sauté the nuts until golden. Drain on paper towels and set aside.

In a medium skillet, heat 1 tablespoon of the oil and sauté the onions and beef until the meat is browned and cooked. Drain away any excess liquid. Stir in nuts, cinnamon, allspice, salt and pepper. Taste and adjust seasonings.

Fry a small bit of the lamb mixture (the dough) and check the seasoning.

Pat half of the lamb mixture into a lightly greased 8-inch square baking dish. Pat the beef mixture (the filling) over the lamb mixture.

Place a sheet of waxed paper on your counter and pat the remaining lamb mixture into an 8-inch square, then flip the paper over on top of the beef layer and press lamb mixture down gently.

With a sharp knife cut through the meat to the bottom of the pan making 1 1/2-inch squares or diamonds. This assures neat pieces after baking.

Drizzle the remaining 1 tablespoon olive oil on the top and bake until the top is light brown and the meat has pulled away from the sides of the pan, 50 to 60 minutes.

Cool at room temperature until needed or cover and refrigerate if made a day ahead.

It can be frozen and reheated for serving. For reheating, brush the top of the kibbeth with melted margarine.

# ⁂ MEAT AND EGGPLANT PIE ⁂

## PASTEL DI CARNE CON MASSA FINA
### Serves 6 to 8

This is another of Linda Forristal's recipes from her book *Bulgarian Rhapsody*—an extraordinary meat and eggplant pie, encased in an incredibly tasty crust.

DOUGH:

- 2 1/2 cups all-purpose flour
- 1/2 teaspoon salt
- 1 tablespoon olive oil
- 11 tablespoons margarine or butter
- 1 tablespoon vinegar
- 1/4 cup sparkling water

FILLING:

- 1 small eggplant
- 1 to 2 tablespoons oil
- 1 medium onion, chopped fine
- 1 1/4 pounds ground beef
- 2 large eggs
- 1/2 to 1 cup finely chopped fresh parsley
- 1 teaspoon salt
- freshly ground pepper
- 1 large egg yolk mixed with 1 tablespoon water, for egg wash

To prepare the dough, sift the flour and salt onto a flat surface and make a well in the middle.

Pour in the oil and butter and using your fingers, rub in the oil and butter until the mixture is mealy. Add the vinegar to the sparkling water and gradually add to the flour mixture. Knead the dough and shape it into a ball. Wrap in plastic wrap and refrigerate while making the filling.

Preheat oven to 350°F.

Thoroughly grease a 12-inch quiche pan or deep dish pie pan.

Prepare the filling: Grill the whole eggplant over an open flame or under the broiler until the skin is blackened and soft. When cool, remove the skin and place pulp in a colander to drain for a few minutes, then chop the eggplant.

In a large skillet, heat the oil and sauté the onion until soft and transparent. Stir in the meat and cook it until it changes color. Remove the meat from the heat and cool it slightly. Add the eggplant, eggs, parsley, salt, and pepper to taste. Mix well and let mixture cool.

On a lightly floured board, roll out a little more than half the dough and place it in the prepared pan. Pour in the filling and spread out evenly.

Roll out the remaining dough and place over filling. Crimp the edges together to seal the pie and brush the upper crust with the egg wash. Using a fork, prick the top crust all over.

Bake until the crust turns golden, approximately 45 minutes to 1 hour. Serve hot.

# ⊰ MOROCCAN CHOLENT ⊱

### DAFINA
### Serves 6 to 8

*"Ye shall kindle no fire throughout your*
*habitations upon the Sabbath day" (Exodus 35:3)*

This dish is also called *Schenna, Hamin(m)*, or *Chamim*.

Writings from Talmudic times stated that eating hot food on
the Sabbath was a good deed. Cholent is a Sabbath dish (a meal
in a pot!) that was born out of this observance. It is prepared on
Friday prior to sundown and cooked overnight, in a very slow
oven (usually the village baker's oven), and brought home and
eaten Saturday for lunch after returning from services. This
provided a hot, hearty meal without violating the commandment against cooking on the Sabbath. Religious Jews do not
carry objects beyond their homes on the Sabbath, so a string or
wire (*eruv*) was/is put around the village or community making
it "one home."

When the Sephardic Jews were expelled from Spain in 1492,
many fled to northwestern Africa across the Straits of Gibraltar.
The hamin was changed, adjusting for local ingredients and
then called dafina (covered) in Morocco. Every family seems to
have its own version, and when you return from Sabbath services it's the first thing you smell upon entering any Sephardic
home. Any other favorite vegetables can be added, and the eggs
can be removed and eaten at any time.

4 tablespoons extra-virgin olive oil

2 large onions, chopped

4 to 6 garlic cloves

2 cans (15 ounces each) chick-peas (garbanzo beans), rinsed and drained

2 beef bones with marrow

3 pounds brisket or chuck roast, cut into 4 pieces

3 pounds small potatoes

2 or 3 sweet potatoes cut into chunks

4 tablespoons honey

1 tablespoon paprika

2 teaspoons ground cumin

1 teaspoon allspice

1/2 teaspoon cinnamon

1/2 to 1 teaspoon ground turmeric

pinch of saffron threads, crumbled

1/2 cup of chopped fresh parsley

salt

freshly ground pepper

4 to 6 large eggs

Preheat oven to 225°F.

In a large pot, heat the oil and sauté the onions and garlic until soft and translucent. Add the chickpeas, bones, meat, potatoes, honey, paprika, cumin, allspice, cinnamon, turmeric, saffron, parsley, and salt and pepper to taste. Add enough water to cover, place the unshelled eggs in the center, and bring to a boil.

Reduce the heat to medium low and simmer for 1 hour. Skim off the foam occasionally. Cover the pot tightly, place in the oven and cook overnight, or cook on low on the stove for 5 to 6 hours, or until meat is tender and done.

In the morning, after cooking all night, check the water level. If there is too much water, turn the oven up to 250°F or 300°F, cover, and continue cooking. If there is no water, add another cup, cover, and continue cooking.

To serve, place the chickpeas and cooking liquid in one bowl, and the eggs, potatoes, and meat in separate bowls.

# ⊰ SEPHARDIC STUFFED CABBAGE ⊱

*Serves 6*

It is believed that stuffed cabbage leaves originated in the Middle or
Near East as an alternative to using grape leaves. Every country
from Greece to Persia to Egypt has a version of this recipe. After
this idea spread, it became very popular with Eastern European
Jews.

| | |
|---|---|
| *1 large or 2 small heads cabbage* | SAUCE: |
| *(12 to 15 leaves)* * | *3 tablespoons olive oil* |
| *2 tablespoons olive oil* | *1 medium onion, minced* |
| *1 small onion, finely chopped* | *2 garlic cloves, minced* |
| *1/2 cup uncooked white rice* | *1 teaspoon ground cumin* |
| *1 teaspoon ground cumin* | *freshly ground pepper* |
| *1/2 teaspoon turmeric* | *1/2 teaspoon turmeric* |
| *1 pound ground beef (or lamb)* | *2 tablespoons tomato paste* |
| *2 tablespoons chopped fresh* | *2 3/4 cups chicken broth* |
| *parsley* | |
| *freshly ground pepper* | |

Using a small paring knife, cut a 2-inch-deep slit around the
core of the cabbage and remove the core.

Place the cabbage head in a 6-quart pot of boiling salted water.
Cover and cook 10 to 15 minutes or until leaves are soft enough
to fold. Carefully remove 12 to 15 leaves. Drain in a colander or
on a large towel. Save the head of the cabbage and any leaves
still on the head. Carefully remove any hard ribs from the center of the leaves with a sharp paring knife.

Heat the oil in a skillet and sauté the onion until transparent.
Add the rice and cook, stirring for a minute or two.

In a large bowl, combine the onion, rice, cumin, turmeric, meat, parsley, and pepper to taste.

Place a heaping spoon of the filling in the center of each leaf and make a package by folding the stem end (side with rib) over first, then the side opposite the stem and enclose by folding over the sides. Roll them up as tightly as possible.

Lightly grease the bottom of the pot you cooked the cabbage in and line the bottom of the pot with any unused cabbage leaves. Place the stuffed leaves close together in the pot. If more than one layer of stuffed cabbage is needed, separate the layers with cabbage leaves.

Prepare the sauce by heating the oil in a small pot. Sauté the onion and garlic until soft. Add the seasonings and cook for 1 minute.

Mix the tomato paste with 1/4 cup of the chicken broth and add it to the onion mixture. Stir well then add the remaining 2 1/2 cups broth, and cook, stirring for 3 to 5 minutes.

Pour the sauce over the stuffed cabbage.

Place a sheet of foil over the top of the pot, cover the pot with the lid, and simmer, over low heat for 2 to 2 1/2 hours or until meat is cooked and rice tender.

* If desired, you can put the whole cabbage in a plastic bag and freeze it for 2 days before stuffing. To use it, remove cabbage from freezer the night before. Thaw overnight at room temperature. In the morning the wilted leaves will separate easily.

# ⚜ MEATLESS, EGG, AND CHEESE DISHES ⚜

*Sephardic Israeli Cuisine*

# ⊰ BROWN HARD-COOKED EGGS ⊱

*HUEVOS HAMINADOS*
*Makes 8 to 10 eggs*

This dish is popular among the Jews of Turkey and Sephardic Jews of Jerusalem. It is usually used for Sabbath lunch. The long slow cooking gives the eggs a nice color and flavor, especially if they crack during cooking.

*1/4 to 1/3 cup extra-virgin olive oil*

*1 to 2 teaspoons salt*

*1 to 2 teaspoons black pepper*

*outer skins from 4 to 6 onions*

*2 to 3 tablespoons espresso or Turkish instant coffee powder*

*8 to 10 large eggs*

Place 8 to 10 cups of water, oil, salt, and pepper in a large pot.

Place half the onion skins and coffee in the pot. Carefully add the unshelled eggs and cover with the remaining onion skins.

Simmer gently for 6 hours on low heat.

The oil will prevent the water from evaporating too quickly, but more water will have to be added periodically. The egg whites will brown because of the onion skins.

# ⊰ CHICKPEAS AND RICE ⊱

*Serves 4 as a main dish, 6 as a side dish*

2/3 cup uncooked brown rice

2 tablespoons olive oil

1 medium onion, finely chopped

1 or 2 garlic cloves, minced

15-ounce can chickpeas (garbanzo beans), rinsed and drained

2 tablespoons chopped fresh
parsley

1/2 teaspoon dried basil

1/2 teaspoon ground cumin

1/2 teaspoon turmeric

1/2 teaspoon salt

freshly ground pepper

Bring 1 2/3 cups water to a boil in a small saucepan. Add the rice, reduce the heat to low, and cook the rice, covered, until tender, about 35 minutes.

In a large skillet, heat the oil over medium heat and sauté the onion and garlic until tender but not brown. Stir in 1/3 cup of water along with the rest of the ingredients.

Add the cooked rice, mixing well, cover the skillet and simmer over low heat for 15 to 20 minutes. Serve with yogurt and a salad if desired.

# ⊰ CILANTRO PANCAKES ⊱

## PAKORAS
*Makes several dozen, depending on size*

There is a tribe of Indian Jews called Bene Israel and this is one of their dishes.

Serve this with the Cilantro Chutney (page 145).

| | |
|---|---|
| *1 cup dried green peas* | *1/2 teaspoon baking soda* |
| *1 cup mung beans, washed well* | *whole wheat flour, if needed* |
| *1 / 2 teaspoon cumin seeds* | *oil or shortening for frying* |
| *3/4 teaspoon salt* | |
| *1/2-inch piece fresh ginger, peeled* | |
| *1 bunch fresh cilantro, washed and dried* | |

Soak the peas and beans in water for 2 to 6 hours or overnight. Drain well, saving about a cup of the soaking water.

Place beans and peas in a blender or food processor with just enough soaking liquid to help purée, making a thick mixture. More water may be added if needed. Add cumin seeds, salt, ginger, cilantro, and baking soda. Do not add any flour unless the batter is too runny and will not hold a ball shape for frying.

Let the batter sit at room temperature for 1 hour.

In a deep-fat fryer, heat enough oil or shortening to measure at least 2 inches in depth.

Shape mixture into 1-inch balls and drop into hot fat. As they begin to cook, remove the balls from the fat and place on paper towels. Lightly press each ball with a drinking glass to slightly flatten into a pancake shape.

Return pancakes to the hot oil and continue frying until they are golden in color. Drain well on paper towels and serve with Cilantro Chutney.

Balls can be frozen and reheated in a 400°F oven.

# ⌐CILANTRO CHUTNEY⌐

*Makes about 1 cup*

This is another recipe of the Indian Bene Israel and is served with the cilantro pancakes as a condiment, or is used as a sauce with fish or rice.

| | |
|---|---|
| 1 bunch fresh cilantro, washed and dried | 3 tablespoons lemon juice |
| 2 small green chilies or 1/2 teaspoon red chili powder | 1/2-inch piece ginger, chopped |
| | 2 ounces or more plain yogurt |
| 1 teaspoon salt | 1/2 cup flaked coconut (optional) |

In a blender or food processor, combine the cilantro, chilies, salt, lemon juice, ginger, yogurt, and coconut if using. Blend until crunchy. Do not let the mixture turn into a liquid.

Taste and adjust seasonings if necessary. If mixture is too spicy, add more yogurt. If it is not hot enough, add more chilies or chili powder.

Serve with cilantro pancakes, fish, or rice.

# ⊰ EGGPLANTS WITH TOMATO SAUCE ⊱

*IMAN BAYALDI*

*Serves 6*

The story says that a famous Turkish priest or Iman was so delighted with his wife's eggplant creation that he passed out or fainted from pure pleasure, hence the name iman bayaldi "the priest has fainted." Sometimes this dish is referred to as "sultan's swoon." There are many versions of this dish and some include meat. If possible, prepare this a day or two ahead so the flavors can mellow.

6 Asian (long, narrow) eggplants
   or 6 small (6 to 7 inches each)
   baby American eggplants

salt

4 tablespoons olive oil

3 medium onions, peeled and
   sliced thin

6 garlic cloves, finely chopped

3 large tomatoes, peeled, seeded,
   and chopped

1 teaspoon salt

freshly ground pepper

1 tablespoon sugar

1 teaspoon cinnamon

3/4 cup plus 3 tablespoons
   chopped fresh parsley

3 to 4 tablespoons pine nuts
   (optional)

1/2 cup extra-virgin olive oil

juice of 1/2 lemon

Preheat oven to 350°F.

Wash the eggplants, cut off the stem ends and slice them in half lengthwise. With a sharp knife, peel off 1/2-inch strips of skin lengthwise at intervals for a striped effect.

On the pulp (or cut) side, make at least 3 lengthwise slashes, being careful not to pierce the skin on the opposite side.

Sprinkle the eggplants with salt and let them stand for 30 minutes. Rinse with cold water, dry, and turn them over on paper towel to drain well.

Heat 2 tablespoons of the oil and sauté the onions and garlic. Add the tomatoes and cook another 2 minutes. Add salt and pepper to taste, sugar, cinnamon, and 3/4 cup parsley, mixing well. Cook for a minute, then remove the pan from the heat and set aside. Stir in nuts if desired.

Heat the remaining 2 tablespoons of oil and sauté eggplants (in batches if necessary) until tender. Turn eggplants several times while sautéeing. A little more heated oil may be needed. Remove eggplants from the pan and place in a shallow baking dish.

Drain the onion mixture and stuff the slashes of the eggplant with it, allowing some of the filling to cover the top of the eggplants. Grind some pepper over the top of each eggplant and sprinkle with the remaining 3 tablespoons parsley.

Whisk together the extra-virgin olive oil, lemon juice, and 1 cup of water. Pour over and around the eggplants. Cover with aluminum foil or a lid.

Bake until eggplants are tender when pierced with a fork, 15 to 20 minutes. Remove the cover for the last 10 minutes of baking.

Remove the pan from the oven and transfer eggplants onto a serving platter. Let them cool to room temperature.

# ⊰ INDIVIDUAL STUFFED PIES ⊱

## *BOYOS, BOREKAS, BUREKS*
### *Makes about 2 dozen*

Filled pastries are an intricate part of Sephardic cooking. Borekas are
very similar to turnovers, empanadas, or knishes, and can be
served as an appetizer or main course. They are served for a
Sabbath breakfast or a light lunch in many Sephardic homes, and
can be made with many different fillings. They freeze beautifully
and can be reheated.

*1 teaspoon yeast*
*3 1/2 cups all-purpose flour*
*1/4 teaspoon salt*
*oil*
*1 tablespoon grated Parmesan cheese plus additional for topping*

Prepare the dough by dissolving the yeast in 1/2 cup lukewarm
water. Stir in 3 cups flour, the salt, and remaining 1/2 cup lukewarm water, then knead thoroughly and allow the dough to
rest for 10 minutes, covered.

Divide the dough into 4 equal parts and knead each part on a
lightly floured surface until smooth. Place each part into a pan
filled with enough oil to just cover the bottom.

Turn the dough over once in the oil and cover with waxed
paper.

Let dough stand for another 20 minutes.

Preheat oven to 400°F.

On a lightly oiled work surface, place 1 part of the dough and stretch it gradually until it is about 15 inches square. Mix the remaining 1/2 cup flour with 1 tablespoon cheese. Sprinkle the dough with the cheese mixture and fold both ends towards the middle. Sprinkle the dough again with the cheese mixture and fold the dough in half.

Cut into 6 portions and set aside until all sections of the dough have been worked in this manner. Stretch each portion into a 5-inch square and place about 1 tablespoon of the desired filling in the center. Fold each point of the square towards the center, overlapping the points.

Place on a well greased baking sheet and sprinkle the tops with cheese.

Bake until golden brown, 10 to 20 minutes.

SPINACH FILLING

> 2 packages (10 ounces each) frozen chopped spinach, defrosted and drained well
>
> 1 1/2 cups grated Parmesan cheese
>
> 1 large egg, lightly beaten
>
> salt
>
> 1 tablespoon all-purpose flour

Combine all the ingredients in a large bowl and mix well.

*Continued on next page.*

*Continued from page 149.*

## POTATO FILLING

*3 medium potatoes, peeled, cooked, and mashed*
*1/2 cup cottage cheese*
*1 cup grated Parmesan cheese*
*1 teaspoon salt*
*freshly ground pepper*
*2 large eggs*

Combine the ingredients in a large bowl and mix well.

## PUMPKIN FILLING

*2 pounds pumpkin, cooked, drained, and mashed*
*1 cup grated Parmesan cheese*
*2 large eggs, lightly beaten*
*1 teaspoon sugar*
*salt*

Combine pumpkin and cheese. Stir in eggs, sugar, and salt, mixing well.

## CHEESE FILLING

*1 large egg, lightly beaten*
*5 ounces Parmesan or feta or a combination of both, grated*
*8 ounces cream cheese, softened to room temperature*
*freshly ground pepper*

Combine all the ingredients, mixing well.

# ◅ QUICK BOYOS ▻

*Makes about 4 dozen*

This is a much quicker, easier way to prepare *borekas* (Individual Stuffed Pies, page 148), and the end result tastes great.

*2 cans thick flaky biscuits (10 in each can)*
*potato, cheese or other favorite filling (pages 149-150)*
*1 large egg mixed with 1 teaspoon water (egg wash)*
*sesame seeds and/or 1/4 cup grated Parmesan cheese*

Separate each biscuit into 2 or 3 pieces horizontally and place them in a greased baking pan. Let them rest for 30 minutes to relax the dough.

Preheat oven to 400°F.

Stretch each biscuit into an approximately 5-inch circle.

Fill each piece with a heaping tablespoon of any filling and fold the circles in half, forming a half moon shape. Gently press down the edges to seal, then press the edges with the tines of a fork. Place on a lightly greased baking pan.

Brush the top of each pastry with the egg wash, sprinkle with sesame seeds and/or cheese, and bake for 10 to 15 minutes or until lightly browned.

These can be frozen after cooking and cooling to room temperature.

Reheat by placing frozen boyos in a preheated 350°F oven and baking for about 20 minutes or until hot.

# ⊰ POTATO AND LEEK PATTIES ⊱

*Makes about 15 patties*

Leeks resemble oversize scallions but have a milder flavor with a
nutty sweetness. Only use the white and pale green parts.

*1 1/2 cups cold mashed potatoes
(about 2 medium)*

*1 small onion, finely chopped*

*1 or 2 garlic cloves, finely
chopped*

*1/4 cup plus 2 tablespoons all-
purpose flour*

*2 large eggs, lightly beaten*

*2 1/2 tablespoons butter or
margarine, melted and cooled*

*3 to 4 medium-size leeks, mostly
whites with a small amount of
green, roots removed*

*salt*

*freshly ground pepper*

*canola oil for frying*

In a large bowl mix together the mashed potatoes, onion, garlic,
flour, eggs, butter, and 1/4 cup water. Mix well and let mixture
rest for about 30 minutes.

Remove the tough outer leaves from the leeks then wash and
soak the leeks to remove all dirt and grit. Slice the leeks into 1-
inch pieces and boil in water for 5 minutes. Remove from the
pot and immediately place them in a bowl of ice water to stop
the cooking.

Squeeze out the excess water, chop the leeks, and add them to
the potato mixture and mix well. Add salt and freshly ground
pepper to taste.

In a large skillet, heat enough oil to cover the bottom of the pan
and place large spoonfuls of the leek mixture into the hot oil.
Cook until brown on the bottom, then turn the patties over and
cook until firm and brown on the top.

Drain well on paper towels and serve.

NOTE: For Passover just substitute matzo meal for the flour.

# ⚜SHOU SHOU'S FRESH HERB KUKU ⚜

*Serves 6*

A special version of an omelet that is very popular in Iran.

6 large eggs

2 tablespoons flour

salt (optional)

freshly ground pepper

3 cups finely chopped fresh
  parsley

1 to 3 cups finely chopped fresh
  scallions, mostly whites with
  a little green

1/2 cup chopped fresh dill

1/2 cup chopped fresh cilantro

1/2 cup chopped walnuts

1/2 cup dried cranberries

1 medium potato, cooked, peeled,
  grated or mashed

1/2 cup vegetable oil

Preheat oven to 350°F.

Mix the eggs, flour, salt if desired, and pepper to taste, beating well. Stir in the parsley, scallions, dill, cilantro, walnuts, cranberries, and potato.

Pour 1/4 cup of oil into an 8 or 9-inch baking dish or pie pan and place it in the oven for 10 to 15 minutes. Pour in the egg mixture and bake, uncovered, for 30 minutes.

Remove the dish from the oven and carefully pour the remaining 1/4 cup oil over the kuku. Return the dish to the oven and continue baking for another 20 to 30 minutes or until kuku is golden brown.

NOTE: The kuku can also be cooked on top of the stove by heating the oil in a nonstick skillet, pouring in the egg mixture and then cooking, covered, over low heat until it is set (about 25 minutes). Cut the kuku into wedges and turn them over one by one, adding more oil if needed, and cook them covered for another 20 minutes or until golden brown.

# ⇥ ULI'S FALAFEL ⇤

*Makes about 6 dozen, depending on size.*

Uli Zamir makes fabulous falafel, using the family recipe that was handed down from his father Shlomo. Shlomo sold falafel for 20 years from his kiosk in Kiryat Tiv'on.

This recipe is from the cookbook *Meanleaniyumm*, written by well-known Canadian author Norene Gilletz.

| | |
|---|---|
| 1 pound dried chickpeas (about 2 1/4 cups) | 5 to 6 garlic cloves, minced |
| | 1 teaspoon salt |
| 2 slices bread | freshly ground pepper |
| 1/2 cup minced fresh parsley | 3/4 teaspoon cumin |
| 1 bunch fresh cilantro, minced | 1 teaspoon baking soda |
| 1 onion, chopped fine | oil for frying (optional) |

Clean the chickpeas by placing them in a strainer or colander and rinsing thoroughly. Soak chickpeas in 8 cups cold water for 24 hours (at room temperature). Drain chickpeas and set aside.

Soak the bread in a little water, but don't squeeze it completely dry.

Grind the chickpeas in a blender or processor until fine. Place chickpea mixture in a large bowl.

In a processor or blender, grind the parsley, cilantro, onion, garlic, and bread together until fine. Add the chickpeas and mix well to blend. Add seasonings and baking soda.

Mixture will be thick, but add a little water (1/3 to 1/2 cup) so that mixture is moist but still holds together.

Shape mixture into 1-inch balls.

Deep-fry the falafel in hot oil until crisp and golden—they will float to the surface when done. Drain well on paper towel. These can be frozen and they reheat well.

NOTE: Noreen suggests an alternative to frying for those who want to watch their calories. Place the oven rack in the lowest position in the oven. Preheat oven to 450°F and line 2 baking sheets with aluminum foil sprayed lightly with nonstick spray and then brushed lightly with a little oil. Bake uncovered for 10 minutes or until the bottoms are brown. Carefully turn falafel over and bake another 8 to 10 minutes.

*Sephardic Israeli Cuisine*

# ❧ VEGETABLES ☙

*Sephardic Israeli Cuisine*

# ❧ FAVA BEANS WITH LEMON AND GARLIC ❧

*Serves 4 to 6*

3/4 pound large fava beans, soaked overnight in enough water to cover

2 to 3 garlic cloves, peeled and chopped fine

1 teaspoon salt

1/2 cup fresh lemon juice

1 teaspoon cumin (optional)

1 to 2 tablespoons extra- virgin olive oil

1/2 cup finely chopped fresh cilantro or parsley

Place the beans in a bowl and soak overnight in enough water to cover.

Drain the beans, place them in a pot and cover them with fresh water. Bring to a boil, reduce the heat to simmer, cover, and cook just simmering, until the beans are thoroughly tender (30 minutes to an hour). Make sure the beans are always covered with water. If needed, add a little boiling water from time to time to make up for the water that is absorbed by the beans. Remove the pot from the heat and drain beans well, saving the cooking liquid.

Place the chopped garlic in a bowl with the salt and mash to a paste (or use a mortar and pestle). Stir in the lemon juice and cumin, if using, and mix well.

Remove about 1 cup of beans and with a fork mash them with 1/2 cup of reserved bean cooking liquid. Texture will be like runny mashed potatoes. Stir in the garlic paste. Using a slotted spoon, add the whole beans and mix well. If the mixture is too dry, add a little more of the bean cooking liquid.

Stir in the olive oil and pour mixture onto a deep serving platter. Garnish the platter with parsley or cilantro and serve hot or at room temperature with Flat Bread (page 174) or pita bread (page 173) as a scoop.

# ⚜ MOROCCAN SWEET CARROTS ⚜

*Serves 4*

Another family recipe from Judith Amrani.

*1/3 cup honey*
*1/4 cup lemon juice*
*8 to 10 carrots, peeled and shredded*
*1 /2 cup raisins (optional)*
*1 tablespoon orange flower water*

Dissolve the honey in the lemon juice. Add the carrots and the raisins, if desired, and mix well.

Sprinkle with orange flower water and let carrots sit an hour or longer before serving or cover and refrigerate until serving. The longer it marinates the better it gets.

# ⌐ OKRA ⌐

## BAMYA or BAMIA
### Serves 4

There is a story that when King Solomon was preparing a welcoming feast for the Queen of Sheba he wanted 100 dishes served. His chef could only think of 99 and went out in the fields to look for inspiration. There, for the first time, he noticed the okra pod and named it *bamia* (for *ben maiyah*, which means "the hundredth").

*1 pound fresh or frozen okra*

*2 medium onions, chopped*

*2 tablespoons extra-virgin olive oil*

*1 teaspoon salt*

*1 tablespoon lemon juice*

*4 medium tomatoes, coarsely chopped*

Preheat oven to 400°F.

If you are using fresh okra peel off the outer layer around the crown. Cut off the bottom tip, wash the okra and drain well.

Place the okra in a saucepan with the onions, oil, salt, lemon juice, and tomatoes. Cover and simmer on low until tender.

Place vegetables in a shallow baking dish and bake, uncovered until nicely browned, about 30 minutes.

# ⊰ SPINACH BAKE ⊱

*Serves 6 to 8*

According to Daniela Sciaky, this dish can be made with eggplant, squash, or whatever vegetable you think would work! It can be used as a filling in dough (called *pastel de sfongato*) or eaten between two slices of toast as a sandwich. This is also a good Passover dish, since spinach is a Passover staple for the Sephardic Jews.

1 pound small curd creamy cottage cheese

2 boxes (10 ounces each) frozen chopped spinach, defrosted and wrung out

3 to 4 ounces feta cheese, crumbled

3 large eggs, slightly beaten

1 1/2 tablespoons bread crumbs or matzo meal

Preheat oven to 350°F.

In a large bowl combine all the ingredients, mixing well.

Lightly grease a 9 by 11-inch baking pan and spread the spinach mixture in the pan. Bake for 1 hour or until set.

# ⊰ SWEET COUSCOUS ⊱

*Serves 8 to 10*

Couscous is the national "dish" of Morocco and most North African countries. Couscous means rolled grains of semolina and is made from hard durum wheat, with each grain separated from the other. In Moroccan homes, couscous is eaten with the hand. Sweet couscous is served at the end of a Moroccan meal, before the fruit is passed around to "aid the digestion."

| | |
|---|---|
| 2 tablespoons olive oil | 4 ounces slivered almonds |
| 7 cups couscous | 1/4 cup orange flower water |
| 1 tablespoon salt | 1/4 cup granulated sugar |
| 1/4 cup butter or margarine in small pieces, at room temperature | 1/4 cup confectioners' sugar |
| | 1 to 2 teaspoons ground cinnamon |

Bring 8 cups water to a boil with the olive oil and stir in the couscous and salt. Cover the pot and remove it from the heat. Let sit 10 minutes, or until all the water is absorbed.

Fluff the couscous with a fork and place it in a large bowl. Stir in the butter or margarine, almonds, orange flower water, and granulated sugar.

Mix well and sprinkle with confectioners' sugar and cinnamon.

# ⚜ SWEET RICE WITH NUTS ⚜

*Serves 8 to 10*

1 teaspoon saffron threads

3 tablespoons hot water

3 cups plus 1 tablespoon
  uncooked long grain rice

3/4 cup to 1 cup sugar

1/4 cup rose or orange flower
  water

2 heaping tablespoons sliced
  blanched almonds

2 heaping tablespoons skinned
  pistachios

Crumble the saffron threads in the hot water and let sit for about 30 minutes, then drain well.

Bring 6 cups of water to a boil and stir in the rice, cooking on low heat, partially covered, for 25 minutes.

Stir in the saffron, sugar, rose water, and almonds and simmer for 10 minutes.

Stir in the pistachios, mixing well.

Serve warm or chilled.

# ⊰ ZUCCHINI WITH SAUCE ⊱

## ENGINARA
### Serves 6

The majority of Jews who settled in Bulgaria came from Spain in the
fifteenth century seeking refuge from the Inquisition. There they
enjoyed a privileged status due to their education and skills and
provided a Spanish influence to Bulgarian Jewish cuisine. The
Ladino word *enginara* conveys the idea of a light, cold dish. This
recipe is courtesy of Linda Forristal from her book *Bulgarian
Rhapsody*.

| | |
|---|---|
| 2 pounds zucchini | freshly ground pepper |
| 2 teaspoons olive oil | 1/4 teaspoon ground coriander |
| juice of 1 large lemon | 1 sprig parsley, whole |
| 1 teaspoon sugar | 1 stalk celery, whole |
| 1/2 teaspoon salt | 1/2 cup finely chopped fresh dill |

Wash zucchini and cut off the ends. Do not peel. Slice zucchini
lengthwise into pieces 1/4-inch thick. If zucchini are extra long,
slice them in half crosswise.

In a medium pot place 1/2 cup water, the olive oil, lemon juice,
sugar, salt, pepper to taste, coriander, parsley, and celery.

Add the sliced zucchini, cover, and simmer on low heat until
the zucchini is almost cooked, about 10 minutes.

Using a perforated ladle, remove the zucchini, drain, and neatly
arrange it in the bottom of a serving dish.

Strain the remaining liquid, return it to the pot, and simmer on
low heat until reduced by half.

Pour the sauce over the zucchini and sprinkle with chopped dill.

Refrigerate before serving.

Serve cold.

*Sephardic Israeli Cuisine*

# ❧ BREADS ❧

*Sephardic Israeli Cuisine*

# ⊰ BASIC PITA ⊱

*Serves 6*

This is the most popular bread in Israel and the Middle East. It is served with every meal.

*2 teaspoons dry yeast*

*1 cup warm water*

*3 cups all-purpose flour*

*1 teaspoon salt*

Dissolve the yeast in the water.

Sift together the flour and salt and stir into the yeast and water. Work the mixture into ball and knead for several minutes, adding extra water or flour if needed.

Place dough in a lightly greased bowl, cover the bowl with a damp cloth and let dough rise in a warm place until doubles in size, about 1 hour.

Preheat the oven to 350°F.

With lightly floured hands, divide the dough into 6 equal portions and roll into balls. With either your hand or a rolling pin, pat and press each ball of dough into a 5-inch circle, each about 1/2 inch thick. Place on an ungreased baking sheet and bake for 10 minutes, or until the pita are light golden brown.

Cool on a wire rack, and when breads are at room temperature cut a slit at one end if you are going to fill them.

# ⊰ FLAT BREAD ⊱

*Makes 12*

Most Sephardic Jews do not bake a special Sabbath challah bread.
Their breads are usually plain in flavor and include Arab flat bread
and pitas. Moroccan Jews do bake a special bread for the Sabbath.
Sephardic Jews use a number of breads on the Sabbath, the usual
number being two, but in ancient times they used as many as
twelve.

| | |
|---|---|
| 1 1/2 teaspoons dry yeast | 2 cups all-purpose flour |
| 1/2 teaspoon sugar | 1/2 teaspoon salt |
| 1/2 cup warm water | 1/4 cup butter, melted and cooled |

Soften yeast with sugar in warm water for 10 minutes, till
foamy.

Place flour and salt in food processor, and when yeast is ready
add it to the flour mixture followed by the cooled butter.
Process for 45 seconds.

Place dough in a lightly greased bowl, turn to grease top of
dough, cover with a towel, and let rise in a warm place until
doubled, about 1 hour.

Divide dough into 12 or 24 portions. Roll each into a ball, flatten with the palm of your hand, and roll to 3 inches diameter
on a lightly floured surface. Place each round on a lightly
greased baking sheet.

Cover with a towel and let rise 10 to 30 minutes.

Preheat oven to 450°F.

Bake for 6 to 8 minutes if you want them soft (so they will
"roll" or "fold") or 13 minutes if you like them hard.

# ⚜ JACKIE BEN EFRAIM'S CHALLAH ⚜

*Makes 2 loaves*

According to Freda Reider in her book *The Hallah Book*, the word *hallah* refers to "a small portion of prebaked dough that the Jews of the Temple period gave as a weekly Sabbath offering to their priests who devoted all their time to ritual, study, worship, and Temple service. According to Jewish law, this dough had to be mixed from wheat, barley, spelt, oat, or rye flour intended specifically for bread and not for cake. The breads were white and sweet. The shape was originally round. When the Temple was destroyed, the bread offering to the priests ceased. To commemorate the ancient law of setting aside hallah, Jews to this day separate a small portion of prebaked dough, which they bless and burn. This small piece of separated dough is now called *'hallah,'* which means *'offering,'* and the sweet white bread itself is now also known as hallah." Traditionally, challah is braided into a long oval shape, but on Rosh Hashanah and Yom Kippur it is coiled into a round.

| | |
|---|---|
| *1 tablespoon yeast* | *pinch of saffron* |
| *1/2 cup plus 1 tablespoon sugar* | *1 large whole egg* |
| *1/2 cup warm water* | *1 egg white* |
| *1/2 cup boiling water* | *1/4 cup cold water* |
| *1/4 cup vegetable oil* | *5 to 6 cups all-purpose flour* |
| *1 teaspoon salt* | *1 egg yolk mixed with 1 teaspoon water (egg wash)* |

Mix the yeast and 1 tablespoon of the sugar and dissolve in the warm water.

Dissolve the remaining sugar in the boiling water, then stir in the vegetable oil, salt, and saffron.

Beat together the whole egg and egg white.

Stir the cold water into the sugar mixture, then add the beaten egg and egg white.

Place the yeast mixture in a large mixing bowl (of an electric mixer) and add the egg mixture, mixing well. Stir in the flour, mixing until dough begins to hold together. Knead dough for 3 minutes in the mixer (or by hand for 10 minutes) and another minute by hand. Place in a lightly oiled bowl, cover, and let rise for an hour in a warm place.

Divide dough into 6 equal parts. With your hands roll each part into a rope about 18-inches long and 3/4-inch thick. Braid 3 ropes together by bringing the left rope under the center rope and laying it down.

Bring the right rope under the new center rope and lay it down. Repeat until the loaf is finished. Braid the other 3 ropes into a loaf. Cover, and let them rise again for another hour.

Preheat oven to 400°F. Brush loaves with the egg wash.

Bake for 5 minutes, then reduce heat to 350°F and bake another 20 minutes or until bread tests done (knock on it and listen for a hollow sound).

Jackie spritzes the challahs with water every 5 minutes while baking, using a plant mister for a nicer crust!

# ⊰ LEBANESE BREAD ⊱

*KHOUBIZ*
*Makes 8 breads*

| | |
|---|---|
| 1/2 ounce dried yeast (2 packets) | 8 cups all-purpose flour |
| 2 1/2 cups lukewarm water | 2 teaspoons salt |
| 1 teaspoon sugar | 3 tablespoons oil |

Dissolve yeast in 1/4 cup of warm water, add sugar, let it sit about 10 minutes, or until foamy.

Sift flour and salt into a large mixing bowl, make a well in the center and pour the yeast into the well. Mix, adding water gradually. Knead until soft dough is formed, then knead until smooth and shiny.

Work 2 tablespoons of the oil into the dough, and roll into a large ball. Pour the remaining oil into a large bowl and roll the dough all around the oil.

Cover bowl with a towel and let rise until double in size, about 1 hour or more.

Punch the dough down and place on a lightly floured surface and knead for 1 or 2 minutes. Divide the dough into 8 pieces and roll each into a ball. Flatten each ball and roll on a lightly floured surface using a rolling pin so that 8 circles are formed, each about 1/4 inch thick.

Place circles on a lightly floured cloth, and cover with another floured cloth. Let dough rise again until nearly double in size, about 25 minutes.

Preheat oven to 450°F and place a cookie sheet in the oven to warm for 5 minutes.

Remove the cookie sheet from the oven and lightly grease it. Place a circle on the sheet and bake until it swells up in the center and browns slightly, 4 to 8 minutes.

Remove each bread from the oven as it cooks and wrap in a kitchen towel. Continue and cook all the breads, which should be white and soft and chewy. When they are cut in half, a pocket will be formed in the middle.

# ⊰ MATZO ⊱

*Makes about 25 small squares or circles.*

Matzo is the unleavened bread used to commemorate and celebrate Passover. In their rush to leave Egypt, the Jews had no time for their bread dough to rise and instead ate unleavened bread, which is why it is eaten at Passover. I like to brush some olive oil mixed with za'atar or salt on top before baking.

*4 cups unbleached all purpose-flour*
*1 to 1 1/2 cups cold water*

Preheat oven to 475°F.

In a large bowl combine flour and gradually add 1 cup water. Add a little more water or flour if needed.

Knead dough with your hands until it is firm and can be gathered into a ball. Break off a piece of dough and roll into a ball the size of a golf ball.

Repeat until all the dough is used. You will have about 25 balls of dough.

On a lightly floured surface, roll out each ball of dough in all directions (to form a circle or square) as thin as possible, and place on an ungreased cookie sheet.

Bake for 6 to 10 minutes or until light brown.

# ⊰ YEMENITE SWEET SABBATH BREAD ⊱

## KUBANEH

*Serves 12*

According to Gil Marks in his book *The World of Jewish Cooking*, Yemenites traditionally "placed this bread in the oven at the lowest temperature on Friday evening just before Shabbat began and let it cook overnight so they could eat it for Shabbat breakfast. Kubaneh is traditionally served at Sabbath lunch with chilbeh (Yemenite fenugreek relish) and hard-boiled eggs."

*1 tablespoon active dry yeast*

*1 1/2 cups lukewarm water*

*3 tablespoons thick jam (apricot, orange, or your favorite)*

*4 to 5 cups all-purpose flour*

*1 tablespoon salt*

*3 tablespoons butter or margarine, melted*

*hard-cooked eggs (1 per person) (optional)*

*2 or 3 large tomatoes, sliced (optional)*

Dissolve the yeast in the lukewarm water, and stir in the jam. Let the mixture sit for 5 minutes.

Place 4 cups of the flour and the salt in your mixing bowl and make a well in the center. Pour the yeast mixture into the well. Using the dough hook on your mixer, mix the dough until it is kneaded.

Place the dough in a lightly oiled bowl, cover with a clean kitchen towel, and let rise for 1 hour.

Punch dough down, remove the dough, place on a work surface, and knead in as much of the remaining cup of flour that is needed to make a smooth but slightly sticky dough. Return the dough to the bowl, cover, and let rise for another hour.

Rub some of the melted butter or margarine around the inside of a heavy 5- to 6-quart pot.

Punch down the dough and divide into 4 balls. Roll the balls around in the remaining melted butter or margarine and place in the bottom of the pot. Cover with the lid and let rise for 30 minutes.

Preheat the oven to 375°F. Place rack in the lowest position in the oven.

Bake the bread covered in the pot for 30 minutes. Reduce heat to 150°F (or your oven's lowest temperature) and continue baking overnight or for at least 8 hours.

Serve hot for breakfast by pulling off pieces and if desired, serve with eggs and sliced tomatoes.

*Sephardic Israeli Cuisine*

# ❧ DESSERTS ❧

# ⚜ ALMOND MACAROONS ⚜

*Makes about 24*

8 ounces blanched almonds

1 cup granulated sugar

pinch of salt

2 large egg whites

1/2 teaspoon almond extract

2 tablespoons confectioners' sugar

In a food processor combine the almonds, granulated sugar and salt. Grind them together as fine as possible.

Beat the egg whites stiff, but not dry, and add the almond extract toward the end of the beating. Carefully fold in the almond sugar mixture.

Line a cookie sheet with parchment paper, or lightly grease and flour a cookie sheet.

Using your hands, pinch off pieces of the almond mixture about the size of a walnut and shape with your hands to form a ball with a pointy top.

Sift the confectioners' sugar over the tops of the macaroons, and let the macaroons sit at room temperature for about 2 hours to dry out before baking.

Preheat oven to 300°F and bake macaroons for about 25 minutes, or until they just begin to turn light brown.

# ⊰ BAKLAVA ⊱

*Makes about 30 pieces*

| | |
|---|---|
| approximately 2 cups butter or margarine, melted (vegetable oil can be used) | 3 to 4 cups coarsely chopped almonds (not blanched), with skin if desired |
| 4 cups sugar | juice of 1/2 lemon |
| 2 to 3 teaspoons cinnamon | grated rind of 1 lemon |
| 1 pound phyllo dough, at room temperature | grated rind of 1 orange |
| | 1 cinnamon stick |

Preheat the oven to 350°F.

Grease the bottom and sides of a 9 by 13-inch baking pan with some of the melted butter.

Mix 1 cup of the sugar with the cinnamon and set aside.

Place 1 sheet of phyllo into the pan and brush thoroughly with melted butter, then lay another sheet of phyllo on top, brush with butter, and repeat the process until you have used 5 sheets.

Sprinkle the fifth sheet with about 3 tablespoons of the chopped almonds and 1 tablespoon of the sugar/cinnamon mixture. Then place another sheet of phyllo on top, and brush with melted butter. Place another sheet of phyllo on top, and sprinkle with about 3 tablespoons nuts and sugar mixture.

Repeat the procedure, spreading the phyllo sheets alternately with the nuts and sugar, then the melted butter until you have only 5 phyllo sheets left.

The last 5 sheets should be brushed with melted butter and layered on top, but leave the top sheet dry (no butter) and sprinkle it with cold water.

Bake the baklava for 45 minutes. Remove the pan from the oven and cool slightly on a wire rack.

With a sharp knife, cut diagonally two thirds of the way through the baklava (but not to the bottom), first in one direction, then in the other to form diamond-shaped pieces.

In a large pot, combine the remaining 3 cups sugar, 1/2 cups water, lemon juice, lemon rind, orange rind, and the cinnamon stick to make the syrup.

Bring mixture to a boil, reduce heat, and cook, stirring for about 10 minutes. Remove from heat and let the syrup cool, removing the cinnamon stick.

Pour syrup over the baklava and chill for an hour or more, and just before serving finish cutting the diamonds all the way down to the bottom so the pieces can be easily removed from the pan.

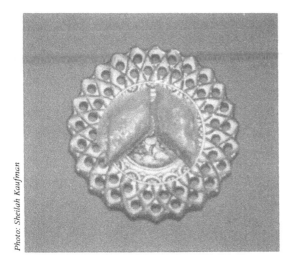

*Photo: Sheilah Kaufman*

# ⚜ BUTTER COOKIES ⚜

*KOURABIEDES*
*Makes about 48*

This cookie is similar to shortbread.

| | |
|---|---|
| 2 cups unsalted butter, softened to room temperature | 1 teaspoon vanilla |
| 3/4 cup confectioners' sugar plus additional for rolling | 1/4 teaspoon almond extract (optional) |
| 1 large egg yolk | 4 1/2 cups sifted all-purpose flour |
| 1 tablespoon milk | 1 teaspoon baking powder |

Preheat oven to 350°F.

Cream together butter and 3/4 cup sugar, mixing well. Add egg yolk, milk, vanilla, and almond extract (if desired) and continue beating until batter is light and fluffy.

Add the flour and baking powder slowly on the lowest speed of the mixer, mixing until a soft ball of dough that is not sticky is formed. If needed, cover the dough and refrigerate for 1 hour.

Break off pieces of dough the size of a walnut and flatten into a circle.

Place on a greased baking sheet and bake until golden, about 20 minutes. Do not let them brown.

Cool and roll in confectioners' sugar.

# ⊰ BUTTER RING COOKIES ⊱

*Makes about 40 cookies*

These dry, not very sweet cookies, somewhat like shortbread, are usually served with coffee or milk or eaten plain. Cookies using similar dough are very common throughout the Middle East.

*1 cup sugar*
*1 cup butter*
*3 cups all-purpose flour*
*slivered almonds or chopped pistachios (optional)*

Preheat oven to 350°F.

In a mixing bowl cream together the sugar and butter.

Slowly add enough flour to hold the mixture together. If dough remains mealy, slowly add a tablespoon or more of melted, cooled butter. When dough holds together, shape it into a ball.

Break off walnut-size pieces of dough and gently roll each piece back and forth in the palms of your hands until you have a "rope" about 4 inches long. Press both ends together to form a ring, and if desired, place a sliver of almond there, or sprinkle the tops with chopped pistachio nuts.

Bake for 10 to 12 minutes until bottoms are lightly browned. Cookies should remain white when they have finished baking.

Cool on a wire rack.

# ⊰ CHOCOLATE SALAMI ⊱

*Makes about 36 pieces*

Rebecca Ets-Hokin, in an article for the *Jewish Bulletin of Northern California,* pointed out that "Chocolate has Jewish roots. After the Inquisition, the Conversos—Portuguese and Spanish Jews who were forced to convert to Christianity but continued to practice Judaism, secretly—were involved in exporting cocoa from South America. They established chocolate factories in Holland and France, beginning in the 1600s." This interesting no-bake cookie is so named because the slices resemble salami. They are very rich. The recipe is also called Chocolate Mosaic in Jewish homes in Istanbul.

| | |
|---|---|
| 1 pound vanilla wafers | 1 cup margarine |
| 1 cup sweet red wine | 1 teaspoon vanilla |
| 1 1/4 cups sugar | 1 1/2 cups chopped pecans |
| 3/4 cup cocoa or 5 ounces European bittersweet chocolate | 8 marshmallows, cut into small pieces (optional) |

Break the cookies into small pieces.

Combine the wine, sugar, cocoa (or chocolate), and margarine in a pot over medium heat. Stir and cook, mixing well, until the margarine is melted.

Stir in vanilla, nuts, cookies, and marshmallows (if desired).

Form candy mixture into rolls or logs about 2 inches wide and wrap tightly in foil.

Freeze until ready to serve, then slice and keep refrigerated.

# ⊰ COCONUT MACAROONS ⊱

*Makes 24 to 36 cookies*

*3 large egg whites, at room temperature*
*pinch of salt*
*2/3 to 3/4 cup sugar*
*1 3/4 cups shredded, unsweetened coconut*

Preheat oven to 350°F.

Lightly grease 2 cookie sheets.

Using an electric mixer, start the whites and salt on low speed, beating until bubbles form. Turn speed to high and when soft peaks begin to form, gradually add sugar, a small amount at a time until stiff peaks form.

Carefully fold in coconut and drop mixture by heaping table-spoonfuls onto cookie sheets. Leave about 2 inches in between each cookie.

Bake for 10 to 15 minutes or until cookies begin to turn lightly brown.

Remove from oven and cool for a few minutes before removing cookies from the pans.

Let cool completely and store in airtight containers. Cookies may be frozen.

# ⤙ DATES IN PASTRY ⤚

## MENANA

*Makes about 24 pastries*

2 1/2 cups all-purpose flour

1/ 2 cup margarine

1/2 tablespoon sugar

1 tablespoon orange flower water

1/4 to 1/2 cup ice water (you
    may need more)

1 pound pitted dates

1/2 teaspoon cinnamon

1 teaspoon grated orange rind
    (optional)

1/3 cup chopped walnuts
    (optional)

confectioners' sugar

In the food processor combine the flour, margarine, sugar, and
1/2 tablespoon of the orange flower water and process to make a
ball of dough. Add very small amounts of ice water if dough
does not hold together, making a ball.

Place the dates, 1/4 cup water, cinnamon, and 1/2 tablespoon
orange flower water (or orange rind, if desired) in a pot and cook
on low heat, stirring, until mixture resembles a paste. This may
take about 15 minutes or more. Add additional water, a little at a
time, if needed.

Remove mixture from heat and let cool. Stir in nuts if using.

Preheat oven to 350°F.

Pinch off a small ball of dough and flatten the ball between
your hands forming a 3-inch circle, or roll out small amounts of
dough at a time and cut into 3-inch circles. Place a small
amount of filling in the middle and fold one half of the circle
over the filling. Continue using all dough and filling, pressing
edges together to seal.

Place pastries on a cookie sheet and bake for 20 to 25 minutes.

When pastries are cool, roll in confectioners' sugar.

# ⊰ HANUKAH DOUGHNUTS ⊱

## SFENZ
*Makes 6 to 8 doughnuts*

This is the Libyan version of fried Hanukah doughnuts.

| | |
|---|---|
| 2 large eggs, beaten | SYRUP: |
| 2 tablespoons sugar | 2 cups sugar |
| 2 tablespoons vegetable oil | 1/4 teaspoon lemon juice |
| 1 1/2 teaspoons baking powder | 1/4 teaspoon orange flower water |
| 1 cup all-purpose flour | 1/8 teaspoon vanilla |
| rind of one orange, chopped fine (optional) | 1/2 cup chopped almonds or walnuts (optional) |
| 1/4 cup blanched almonds, chopped fine | |
| 1/4 teaspoon orange flower water (optional) | |
| vegetable oil for frying | |

Combine the eggs, sugar, oil, baking powder, flour, orange rind, if using, almonds, and orange flower water in a large bowl to form a firm dough. Add 1 or 2 more tablespoons of flour if needed.

On a lightly floured surface, roll the dough out until it is 1/2-inch thick.

Roll the dough up like a log or jelly roll with a hole in the center. Cut the log into pieces about 2 inches wide to form the doughnuts.

Heat the oil over medium heat until hot then reduce the heat to low. Add the doughnuts a few at a time and fry for 2 to 3 minutes or until lightly browned on each side. The doughnuts will rise to the top when done. Remove from the oil and drain well on paper towels.

Prepare the syrup by combining the sugar, 1 1/2 cups water, lemon juice, orange flower water, and vanilla in a pan. Simmer over low heat for 45 minutes to thicken.

Dip each doughnut into the syrup and place in a colander to drain. If the syrup becomes too thick, add 1 or 2 tablespoons of water. Spread the doughnuts on a serving platter and sprinkle with chopped almonds or walnuts if desired.

*Photo: Vivienne Roumani-Denn*

# ⊰ LEMON CAKE ⊱

*Serves 8*

6 large eggs, separated          juice of 2 lemons (1/2 cup)
3/4 cup sugar                    3/4 cup all-purpose flour
6 tablespoons canola oil         2 teaspoons baking powder
grated rind of 2 lemons          confectioners' sugar (optional)

Preheat the oven to 350°F.

Lightly grease a 9 by 13-inch baking pan.

Using a mixer on medium speed, beat the yolks and sugar for about 5 minutes until thick and lemon colored.

Slowly add the oil, mixing well. Add the lemon rind and slowly add the lemon juice, mixing well to blend. Turn mixer to low and add the flour and baking powder. Mix only to blend well.

Place egg mixture in another bowl and carefully wash and clean the mixing bowl.

Place the whites in the clean bowl and beat on medium speed until eggs are foamy. Turn mixer to high speed and beat the whites until stiff.

Place a third of the beaten whites into the egg yolk mixture and carefully fold them in. Add remaining whites and carefully fold them in.

Pour batter into the prepared cake pan.

Bake for 20 to 25 minutes or until top is lightly browned or cake tests done.

Dust with confectioners' sugar if desired.

NOTE: For Passover: Substitute 1/2 cup potato starch plus 1/4 cup cake meal for the flour.

# ⊰ LEMON SHERBET ⊱

*Serves 6 to 8*

1 3/4 cups sugar
grated rind of 1 1/2 lemons
1/2 cup fresh lemon juice

1/2 cup half-and-half
3 1/2 cups milk

Add each ingredient (whisking) in the order given or the recipe will not work.

In a large bowl mix the sugar and lemon rind. Whisk in the lemon juice, mixing well. Slowly add the half-and-half and milk, whisking until everything is well blended.

Pour into pie pans or freezer trays, cover with foil, and freeze. Stir every 20 to 30 minutes until frozen to break up any crystals that may form.

*Sephardic Israeli Cuisine*

# ⊰ MARZIPAN ⊱

*Makes about 36 balls*

The origins of marzipan are still in doubt. Most people believe it came to Spain with the Arabs. It was the sweet traditionally served to celebrate a birth, wedding, or bar mitzvah. In Israel, they are shaped like flowers and fruits and colored accordingly.

1 1/2 cups whole blanched
   almonds
1 cup sugar
1/4 cup plus 3/4 tablespoons rose
   water

1 teaspoon almond extract
about 1 teaspoon food coloring
   (optional)

In a blender or food processor, grind the almonds until finely chopped but not oily.

Place the sugar and 1/2 cup water in a heavy saucepan and bring to a boil, stirring to melt the sugar. Boil for 15 to 20 minutes or until syrup reaches the soft boil stage (240°F on a candy thermometer). Cool slightly and stir in the almond powder, 3/4 tablespoon of the rose water, and the almond extract, mixing well.

Place mixture onto a lightly greased board and knead it for a few minutes, stirring in the food coloring if desired. Wet your hands with the remaining rose water and tear off a small piece of marzipan, squeeze and roll it between the palms of your hands or flatten and cut it into pieces or shapes. Place in small paper candy cups. Let candy sit a day before serving.

Marzipan can be stuffed in dried fruits and should be stored at room temperature in an airtight container, or in the freezer for up to 6 months.

# ❧ ORANGE WALNUT CAKE ☙

*Serves 10*

The Romans introduced walnuts to Europe, but they were known in Judea and Greece in early biblical times. The orange came to Israel from India and Persia. Orange is derived from the Persian word *narang*, which means fragrant.

*1 cup unsalted butter or margarine, softened to room temperature*

*2 cups granulated sugar*

*4 large eggs*

*1/2 cup orange juice*

*grated rind of 1 orange*

*3 cups all-purpose flour*

*1 teaspoon baking powder*

*pinch of salt*

*1 cup coarsely chopped walnuts*

*confectioners' sugar (optional)*

SYRUP (OPTIONAL):

*1 cup granulated sugar*

*2 teaspoons orange flower water*

Preheat oven to 350°F. Lightly grease and flour a 9-inch Bundt or tube pan.

With your mixer on medium speed, cream the butter until light and fluffy, about 5 minutes. Gradually add the granulated sugar and continue beating. Add the eggs, one at a time, beating well after each addition. Slowly pour in the orange juice and add the rind, mixing well.

Sift together the flour, baking powder, and salt and with the mixer on the lowest speed, slowly add the flour mixture. Add the walnuts and beat for 1 additional minute.

Pour batter into the prepared pan. Bake for 45 to 50 minutes or until cake tests done and is lightly browned and springs back when pressed with your finger.
Place on a wire rack to cool.

If desired, prepare sugar syrup by boiling the granulated sugar and 3/4 cup water together for about 10 minutes and then add the orange flower water. Remove syrup from heat to cool. Prick the top of the cake all over and pour the cooled syrup over the cake slowly.

If you don't wish to use the syrup, the cake may be sprinkled with confectioners' sugar when it has cooled.

# ❧ PRETZEL SHAPED COOKIES ❧

### RESHICAS
*Makes about 3 dozen cookies*

3 large eggs

1/3 cup vegetable oil

1 cup sugar

1/4 cup whipping cream, half-and-half, or water

1 or 2 tablespoons cognac or vanilla (optional)

1 1/2 teaspoons ground cinnamon

4 cups all-purpose flour

3 teaspoons baking powder

1 large egg yolk mixed with 1 teaspoon of water (egg wash)

1/3 cup sesame seeds

Preheat oven to 350°F.

Line 2 cookie sheets with aluminum foil.

In a large bowl beat eggs well with a fork. Add oil, sugar, cream, cognac, and cinnamon, mixing well.

Sift together the flour and baking powder in another bowl.

Add 3 1/4 cups flour, a little at a time, to the egg mixture, beating well after each addition. Knead in as much of the last 1/4 cup of flour as needed until dough is soft but workable. It may be a little sticky.

Pinch off small balls of dough about the size of a walnut and roll them gently between the palms of your hands or on a lightly floured board, using the fingers of both hands to roll the dough back and forth into ropes, each 8 to 10 inches long.

Place ropes on cookie sheets and loop one end over to the middle and press to secure it. Then loop the other end across the first loop and press. They should resemble pretzels, but you can shape them to look like bows, a figure eight, or just rings.

*Sephardic Israeli Cuisine*

Carefully brush each cookie with the egg wash and sprinkle them with sesame seeds.

Bake for 20 minutes or until golden brown. Place on racks to cool.

If desired, when all cookies have been baked, turn off the oven, put the cookies back on the cookie sheets, and place them in the turned-off oven for 10 minutes so they will get extra crisp.

Cool cookies on the cookie sheets and then place in airtight containers.

# ⊰ PURIM ROSES ⊱

*DEBLA*

*Makes 10 roses*

In Libya, this was one of the many popular Purim sweets.

| | |
|---|---|
| *5 large eggs* | SYRUP: |
| *1 teaspoon baking soda* | *2 cups sugar* |
| *2 1/2 to 3 cups all-purpose flour* | *1/4 teaspoon lemon juice* |
| *vegetable oil for deep-frying* | *1/4 teaspoon orange flower water* |
| | *1/8 teaspoon vanilla* |

In a large bowl, beat the eggs. Add the baking soda and 2 1/2 cups of flour, mixing well to form a firm dough. If the dough is too sticky, add more flour.

Sprinkle a little flour over a work surface or pastry board and the rolling pin. Separate the dough into 5 pieces and roll out each piece in paper-thin strips.

Heat the oil in a deep frying pan.

Cut the large strips into strips 2-inch wide and about 12-inches long, and prick the dough with a fork. Carefully begin wrapping the strip around the prong of a wide 2-prong fork while frying it. This forms a "rose." Keep rolling (or coiling) it around itself as it fries and fry until lightly browned. Remove from the oil and drain in paper towel lined colander.

Repeat with remaining dough.

Prepare the syrup by combining the sugar, 1 1/2 cups of water, lemon juice, orange-flower water and vanilla together in a pan. Just cover the mixture with water and simmer over low heat for 45 minutes to thicken the syrup. Stir and remove from the heat.

Use immediately or set aside for later use.

Dip the *debla* into the heated syrup, soaking it well, and drain in a colander. If the syrup becomes too thick, add 1 or 2 tablespoons of warm water.

Place the *debla* on a platter and serve.

Photo: Vivienne Roumani Denn

# ⊰ RICE PUDDING ⊱

*Serves 6*

This is a popular dessert in most Mediterranean countries.

*1/2 cup uncooked long-grain white rice*

*1/2 cinnamon stick*

*3 whole cloves (optional)*

*2 1/2 cups milk*

*1/2 cup half-and-half*

*3/4 cup sugar*

*1 teaspoon rose water*

*1/2 cup chopped pitted dates or golden raisins (optional)*

*ground cinnamon, for garnish (optional)*

*2 tablespoons chopped pistachio nuts, for garnish (optional)*

In a pot, bring 1 cup water to a boil and add the rice, cinnamon stick, and cloves. Stir, reduce heat to medium, cover, and cook rice for about 15 minutes or until the water is almost completely absorbed.

Stir in the milk, half-and-half, and sugar. Mix well, cooking and stirring until pudding begins to thicken, 30 to 40 minutes or until the pudding resembles a thick porridge. Be careful not to overcook or it will become solid when cooled.

Remove cinnamon stick and cloves. Stir in rose water and dates or raisins if desired.

Place in serving dish and top with garnish if desired, then press a piece of plastic wrap directly on the surface of the pudding to prevent a skin from forming.

*Sephardic Israeli Cuisine*

# ⚜ SESAME BRITTLE ⚜

*Makes about 2 pounds*

2 cups hulled white sesame seeds
1 cup sugar
1 cup light corn syrup
2 tablespoons margarine
1 teaspoon baking soda

Preheat oven to 350°F.

Place sesame seeds on a large cookie sheet or jelly roll pan and toast in oven for 15 minutes.

Place seeds in a 3-quart pan. Add sugar, corn syrup, 1/3 cup water, and margarine to the sesame seeds. Bring to a boil stirring constantly over medium heat.

Continue to cook, without stirring, until the temperature reaches 270°F on a candy thermometer or until a small amount of the mixture forms a ball when dropped into very cold water. This can take 15 to 20 minutes or more. The ball should be "plastic" in texture but hold a ball shape.

Grease a jelly roll pan.

Stir the baking soda into the sesame mixture and pour into the jelly roll pan. Spread the mixture with a metal spatula so it is 1/4-inch thick. Cool completely then break into pieces.

# ⊰ NUT CAKE WITH SUGAR SYRUP ⊱

*TISHPISHTI*
*Makes 24 pieces*

This, according to coobook author and Jewish cooking maven Joan Nathan, is a typical celebratory cake for Syrian and Turkish Jews. Hers is one of the best recipes for this delightful treat. This is from her book *Jewish Cooking in America*.

CAKE:

3 cups all-purpose flour
1 1/2 tablespoons sugar
1/2 teaspoon cinnamon
1/2 teaspoon ground cloves
3 cups finely chopped walnuts
1 cup vegetable oil

SYRUP:

1 1/2 cups sugar
juice of 1/2 lemon

1/2 teaspoon cinnamon
for sprinkling

Preheat oven to 350°F. Grease a 9-inch round or square baking pan.

In a large bowl, mix together the flour, sugar, cinnamon, cloves, and nuts. Rub your hands through the mixture until the ingredients are well blended. Make a well in the center and add 1/2 cup water and the vegetable oil. Knead very well. This can also be done in the food processor, making sure you don't over process. There should be some crunch in the walnuts.

Place the dough in the prepared pan and pat it down tight. Cut into about twenty-four 2-inch diamond shapes.

Bake for 1 hour.

Make the syrup by mixing the sugar, 2 cups water, and the

lemon juice in a heavy saucepan. Bring to a boil, then lower the heat, and let the mixture simmer, uncovered, for 1 hour or until it is reduced to one-third of the volume.

When cake is done, pour the syrup over the warm cake. Make sure that the pan is on top of a larger pan lest the syrup spill over. Cut it again into the same diamond shapes. Let it cool, covered with a clean dish towel. With a knife remove onto wax paper and if you like, place in small cupcake liners to serve. Sprinkle with the cinnamon.

# ❧SEPHARDIC PASSOVER❧

# ⊰ FISH IN SALSA ⊱

## PECHE EN SALSA
### Serves 4

This is from the recipe collection of Isabella Sciaky.

2 pounds fillet of bass or cod, cut
  into serving-size pieces
salt
1 cup plus 2 tablespoons matzo
  meal
2 large eggs, lightly beaten

oil for frying
8 ounces walnuts, ground
1 cup red wine vinegar
4 tablespoons vegetable oil

Clean the fish and season with a little salt.

Dip the pieces of fish in 1 cup matzo meal, then in the beaten eggs, and again into the matzo meal.

Place enough oil to cover the bottom of a skillet and fry the fish, turning so it is lightly browned on all sides. Remove the fish from the skillet, wash and dry the skillet.

Combine the nuts, wine vinegar, the 2 tablespoons matzo meal, 1 1/2 cups water, and the oil, mixing well.

Place the nut mixture into the skillet or a pot large enough to hold the fish. Bring mixture to a boil and place the fish into the sauce. Spoon enough sauce over the fish to cover the pieces. Return to a boil and cook a couple of minutes.

Place fish on a serving platter and spoon the sauce over it. Place in refrigerator and chill.

Serve cold.

# ⊰ HAROSET FROM TURKEY ⊱

*Makes about 1 1/2 cups*

Haroset is using during the Passover seder to portray the bricks and mortar the Israelites used to build the Pharaoh's storehouses. Ashkenazic haroset (charoset) is usually made from chopped apples, chopped walnuts, sweet red wine or grape juice, and a dash of cinnamon. Sephardic Jews around the world use many different fruit mixtures. During the holiday it is also used as a spread on matzo.

8 ounces pitted dates
8 ounces raisins, dark or golden
2 cups peeled grated apples
orange juice or wine to moisten
1/2 cup finely chopped nuts

Grind (chop in a processor or blender) all the fruits together.

Moisten with juice or wine.

Stir in nuts.

# ⊰HAROSET OF
# THE ABRAVANEL FAMILY⊱

*Makes about 2 cups*

Stephen Mendes Abravanel told me about various Spanish-Portuguese *minhagim* related to the festival. He offered this recipe for haroset as handed down in his family. His family immigrated to Amsterdam from Portugal via Antwerp in the seventeenth century and from Amsterdam to America in the first half of the nineteenth century. "Also, as explained to me by my grandparents over 50 years ago, the concept is to make the haroset as the Torah quote-'as black as pitch or mortar but sweet as written in Shir Ha Shirim—*shachora ani v'na'va*—I am black and beautiful.' We always served the 'Portuguese haroset' on a small silver filigree plate which further beautified the observance of the commandment *(hiddur mitzvah)*—making the mitzvah of Pesach even more beautiful. This recipe as far as I can tell, is unique among the recipes for haroset that I have seen but with all modesty, is the best haroset I have ever tasted," Stephen said.

| | |
|---|---|
| 1 pound dates | 3 tablespoons cherry jam |
| 1 cup fresh orange juice with pulp, or enough juice to cover dates | 6 ounces almonds, ground very very fine—almost to a powder |
| 3 tablespoons sweet grape wine, Cointreau, or sherry | |

Soak the dates in the orange juice, to soften, for an hour.

Place the dates with the juice into a blender and chop. Blend the dates to as fine as you can—remember it should resemble black tar or mortar.

Remove the dates, place in a bowl and mix with the wine and cherry jam.

Sprinkle the almond powder over the haroset before serving.

# ⊰MEAT AND LEEK PATTIES⊱
## *KIFTICAS DE PRASSA, KEFTIKAS DE PUERO*
### *Serves 8 to 10 as a side dish*

Leeks are one of the oldest known vegetables. They are much loved
by Middle Eastern peoples. This dish is served for Passover and
Rosh Hashanah, and can be adapted as a dish for Hanukah by leaving out the meat. This is another wonderful recipe from Isabella
Sciaky.

*8 very thick leeks, whites only
with a little green, roots
removed*

*1/2 pound ground beef, ground
twice*

*3 large eggs*

*1 teaspoon salt*

*freshly ground pepper*

*matzo meal*

*oil for frying*

*lemon slices, for garnish*

Slice leeks in half the long way and wash thoroughly to remove
all the sand. Chop the leeks and place them in a saucepan with
enough cold water to cover. Bring to a boil, cover, and cook the
leeks until they are tender, about 4 to 5 minutes. Drain the
leeks and let them cool. Squeeze out as much water as possible,
but leave just a little water so the keftikas will not be too dry.

Place leeks in a meat grinder or food processor and grind them
(twice through a meat grinder). (Do not put the leeks in the
refrigerator until you have ground them since it will be impos-
sible to grind them after refrigerating).

Combine the leeks, meat, eggs, salt, and pepper to taste and add
enough matzo meal to form into patties (keftes). They should be
about walnut size, then flatten them with your hands.

In a large skillet or fry pan, heat the oil (enough to at least
cover the bottom of the pan) and fry until they are brown on
each side.

Drain well on paper towels.

Serve with slices of lemon.

NOTE: Viviane's grandmother, Venoutcha Benaroyo (from Bulgaria), made these for Passover for the lunch following the seder night. In Ladino they are called *albondigas de prasa*. In her version, she uses a pound of ground meat with the leeks and seasoning (no other ingredients). The patties are then dipped in eggs and matzo meal and fried.

# ⚜ MOROCCAN SPICY APRICOT LAMB SHANKS ⚜

*Serves 4*

Traditionally, Sephardic Jews eat lamb for Passover in remembrance of the time when a year-old lamb was sacrificed and eaten on the eve of the holiday (this was before the destruction of the second Temple in Jerusalem). Sephardic Jews may eat rice with foods during Passover but Ashkenazic Jews do not. This recipe is from my friend Judy Bart Kancigor's new book of recipes and nostalgic family history, *Melting Pot Memories*.

1 small cinnamon stick

1/4 teaspoon ground nutmeg

1/4 teaspoon ground cloves

1 / 2 teaspoon ground ginger

2 teaspoons black peppercorns

1/4 teaspoon cumin seeds

1/4 teaspoon ground cardamom

1 teaspoon fennel seeds

1 / 2 teaspoon coriander seeds

3 tablespoons olive oil

4 lamb shanks, about a pound each, trimmed of excess fat

kosher salt

12 garlic cloves, peeled

4 small onions, peeled and diced

2 cups chicken broth

20 dried apricots

1 tablespoon chopped fresh thyme

freshly ground pepper

Combine the spices in a spice grinder and grind until fine and well mixed. Measure out 2/3 and reserve the rest for another use.

Preheat oven to 350°F.

Heat 2 tablespoons of the olive oil in a large roasting pan over medium-high heat.

Season the lamb with salt and place in the pan and sear on all sides for about 15 minutes. Remove and set lamb aside.

Turn heat to low and add the remaining 1 tablespoon of oil. Let it get hot then add the garlic and onions. Sauté until lightly browned, stirring often, for about 15 minutes. Pour in the chicken broth, turn up the heat and whisk broth, garlic, and onions plus bits stuck to the bottom of the pan. Stir in the spice mixture and apricots.

Place the lamb back in the pan, cover with foil and roast in oven until the meat is very soft, turning the lamb frequently and basting.

Cook for 2 to 2 1/2 hours. Remove the lamb and degrease the sauce.

Stir in thyme, and salt and pepper to taste. If desired serve with couscous or potatoes.

The peppery flavor of the sauce mellows with cooking, but adjust seasonings to taste.

# ⅍ MOROCCAN SWEET POTATO CAKE ⅏

*Serves 4 to 6*

This recipe doubles easily.

| | |
|---|---|
| *1 pound sweet potatoes, washed and peeled* | *2 large egg whites, at room temperature* |
| *3/4 cup coarsely chopped walnuts* | *1/8 teaspoon cream of tartar* |
| *3/4 cup sugar* | |

Preheat oven to 425°F.

Slice the sweet potatoes and boil them until done. Drain the potatoes and dry them out by placing them in a pan over low heat and stirring them with a wooden spoon until the moisture has evaporated.

Place the potatoes in a bowl and mash them, then stir in the walnuts.

In a small pan over high heat, **make a caramel** by cooking 1/2 cup of the sugar until it begins to turn light brown. Be careful not to let it burn. Quickly pour it into the potato mixture, stirring before it can harden, mixing well.

Place the potato mixture into a lightly greased pie pan and shape it into a dome.

Beat the egg whites on low or medium until they get foamy. Add the cream of tartar and turn speed to high, beating until whites begin to stiffen. Slowly add the remaining 1/4 cup sugar, beating until the whites are stiff and glossy.

Ice the potato dome with the meringue and scatter a few walnuts on top if desired.

Bake just until the meringue begins to lightly brown.

Watch carefully, as it only takes a few minutes.

# ⊰ PASSOVER BREAKFAST FRITTERS ⊱

## BOUMUELOS
### Makes 12 to 15 large boumuelos

Viviane, a fabulous cook, gave me this family recipe. The boumuelos are served for breakfast after the first seder in Bulgaria.

4 to 5 matzo

2 cups sugar

2 large eggs

1/4 teaspoon salt

oil for frying

Break the matzo in small pieces, and soak overnight. In the morning, squeeze out as much of the water as possible.

Prepare sugar syrup by boiling sugar and 1 1/2 cups water together, cooking and stirring for 10 minutes. Set syrup aside.

In a large bowl mix together the matzo, eggs, and salt.

Heat enough oil in a frying pan or electric fryer to cover the bottom.

Drop mixture by teaspoonfuls or tablespoons into a round shape. Fry and turn until brown on both sides, then drain well on paper towels.

Serve with the hot sugar syrup.

# ⊰ PASSOVER FAVA BEAN SOUP ⊱

*Serves 4*

This soup is only made by Sephardic Moroccans and is only served for Passover. But it's so good that you will want to make it year-round!

| | |
|---|---|
| 1/4 cup plus 3 tablespoons olive oil | 4 cups chicken broth |
| 1 1/2 pounds stew beef, cut into 1-inch cubes | 2 or 3 medium white potatoes, washed, peeled, and cut into 1-inch cubes |
| 3 tablespoons olive oil | 1/2 teaspoon turmeric |
| 2 large onions, chopped | freshly ground pepper (white preferred) |
| 6 celery leaves, washed and dried | |
| 3 leeks, white part only, washed well and sliced | 1/2 cup chopped fresh cilantro (or more) |
| 1 pound frozen fava beans, defrosted and skins removed | |

In a large skillet, heat 1/4 cup of the olive oil and brown the meat on all sides. Remove the meat from the skillet and set aside.

In a large pot heat the remaining 3 tablespoons of oil and sauté the onion until soft. Add the celery leaves, leeks, and beans and sauté, stirring, for 2 to 3 minutes. Add 3 cups of chicken broth, potatoes, turmeric, and pepper, and bring to a boil. Reduce heat to simmer, cover, and cook until potatoes are soft (30 to 40 minutes).

Remove soup from the stove and let cool enough to handle. Do not process if the vegetables and liquid are hot or the lid will blow off from the pressure of the steam. Pour the vegetables and some of the liquid into a food processor and pulse until vegetables are chunky.

Return the soup to the pot and add the browned meat and the remaining 1 cup of chicken broth.

Cover and simmer another 20 to 30 minutes, then stir in the cilantro and additional pepper if desired.

# ⊰ PASSOVER SPINACH BAKE ⊱

### *MINA*
#### *Serves 6 to 8*

4 pieces matzo, broken into small
   pieces
5 large eggs
salt
freshly ground pepper
1 cup grated cheddar cheese

1 cup grated Parmesan cheese
2 boxes (10 ounces each) frozen
   chopped spinach, defrosted
1 large boiled potato, peeled,
   and mashed
3 large eggs, beaten

Preheat oven to 350°F. Lightly grease a 10-inch deep-dish pie pan.

Place the pieces of matzo in a large bowl and cover with cold water.

Soak the matzo until soft, about 20 minutes. Carefully squeeze out all the excess water and mix with 2 eggs lightly beaten, salt, and pepper to taste. Place half the matzo mixture in the bottom of the prepared pan.

In a bowl combine the two cheese, mixing well.

Squeeze the water out of the spinach and place in a large bowl with 1 1/2 cups of the combined cheeses, the mashed potato, the remaining 3 beaten eggs, and freshly ground pepper.

Spoon the spinach mixture over the matzo mixture in the pie pan.

Top with remaining matzo mixture, and sprinkle with remaining 1/2 cup cheese.

Bake for 30 minutes or until top is golden brown.

*Sephardic Israeli Cuisine*

# ⚞ PASSOVER SPONGE CAKE ⚟

## PAN DE ESPANA PARA PESAH

*Serves 12*

12 large eggs, separated, at room
   temperature

2 cups sugar

grated rind and juice of 1 lemon

grated rind and juice of 1 orange

1/2 cup potato starch

1/2 cup cake meal

Preheat oven to 350°F.

Place the whites in a mixing bowl and begin to beat slowly. As bubbles begin to form, turn mixer speed to high and slowly begin to add sugar. Continue beating until whites are stiff, glossy, and hold a peak. Set aside.

In another mixing bowl, beat the yolks for 5 minutes, then add the grated rind and juice of the lemon and orange.

Take at least a cup of beaten whites and fold carefully into the yolks, then fold in remaining beaten whites.

Sift together the potato starch and cake meal. Sprinkle the mixture over the top of the egg mixture and carefully fold in until blended.

Place cake batter in an ungreased 10 or 12-inch angel pan and bake for about 1 hour or until a cake tester inserted in the center comes out clean and cake is lightly browned.

*Sephardic Israeli Cuisine*

# ⚜ASHKENAZIC CONTRIBUTIONS⚜

# ⊰ BABKA ⊱

## Serves 12

5 to 6 cups all-purpose flour

1/2 ounce dried yeast (2 packets)

1 1/2 cups plus 2 tablespoons sugar

1/4 cup warm water

1 teaspoon salt

3/4 cup butter or margarine, melted

1 cup milk

1/4 cup canola oil

3 large eggs, slightly beaten

1 teaspoon cinnamon

1/2 cup chopped walnuts (optional)

1/2 cup golden raisins

1/2 cup chocolate chips (optional)

1 large egg yolk mixed with 1 tablespoon water (egg wash)*

Place 3 cups of the flour in a large mixing bowl, making a well in the middle.

Dissolve the yeast mixed with the 2 tablespoons of the sugar in the warm water.

Pour yeast mixture into the well and add 1 cup of the sugar and the salt. Mix together thoroughly.

Melt 1/2 cup of the butter in the milk, remove it from the heat, and stir in the oil. Add the butter mixture to the flour, a little at a time, alternating with the eggs.

Beat in another 2 or 3 cups of flour (or more if needed) until mixture is not sticky.

On a lightly floured surface, knead the dough for about 10 minutes, or until smooth.

Lightly oil a large bowl, and roll the ball of dough around until all sides are covered with a little oil. Place a kitchen towel over the bowl and let the dough rise in a warm place until it has doubled in size, about 1 hour. Punch the dough down and place on the counter or a pastry board. Cover the dough and let it rest for 10 minutes.

Divide the dough into 4 parts and roll each part out into a rectangle about 12 inches long by 8 inches wide and 1/8-inch thick. Melt the remaining 1/4 cup butter. Brush rectangles with melted butter and sprinkle them with the 1/2 cup sugar mixed with the cinnamon, nuts, raisins, and chocolate chips if desired.

Roll each rectangle up the long way (like a jelly roll) and place in a greased Bundt or 10 or 12-inch angle food cake pan. Cover with a towel and let dough rise again until doubled in size, 30 to 60 minutes.

Preheat oven to 325°F.

Brush the top of the babka with the egg wash and bake for 1 hour.

Remove from the oven and cool on a wire rack.


*The egg mixture gives the babka a crispy crust. For a softer crust use melted butter instead of the egg mixture.

# ⊰ BLINTZES ⊱

*Serves 6*

Take your choice of two flavorful fillings, and serve these for breakfast, lunch, or a light dinner.

BLINTZES:

4 large eggs

2/3 cup milk

2 tablespoons canola oil

1/2 teaspoon salt

1 1/3 cups all-purpose flour

1/4 cup butter or margarine, melted (for initial cooking)

1 to 2 tablespoons butter or margarine (for final cooking)

CHEESE FILLING:

12 ounces creamed cottage cheese

2 tablespoons sugar

1 teaspoon cinnamon

1 teaspoon grated lemon rind

pinch of salt

1 cup golden raisins

POTATO FILLING:

4 tablespoons butter or margarine

2 or 3 large onions, finely chopped

3 cups mashed potatoes

salt

freshly ground pepper

To prepare blintzes, beat the eggs well in a medium-size bowl or in the food processor. Add the milk, 2/3 cup water, the oil, salt, and flour, stirring well. Let the mixture stand at room temperature for 1 or 2 hours.

Place a 7 or 8-inch crepe pan or blintz pan over medium heat for 2 or 3 minutes. Brush the pan with a little melted butter. Lift the pan from the heat and add enough batter to cover the bottom (about 3 tablespoons); tilt the pan to spread the batter evenly.

Cook the blintz over medium heat until it is slightly golden on the bottom. Turn it over and cook the other side in the same way—do not let it brown. Slide the blintz from the pan onto a dish and cover it with a towel to keep it warm.

Brush the pan with melted butter and repeat the process until all the batter is used.

To make the cheese filling, place the cottage cheese in a strainer or colander and shake out all the excess liquid. Combine the cheese with the remaining filling ingredients in a small bowl.

To make the potato filling, melt the butter in a large skillet and sauté the onions until soft but not brown. Combine the sautéed onions with the mashed potatoes, salt and pepper to taste in a medium bowl.

To fill the blintzes, place 2 to 3 tablespoons of the desired filling in the center of each blintz. Fold the sides into the center and then fold the other two sides into the center to make a neat rectangular package.

Filled blintzes may be refrigerated or frozen at this point.

A few minutes before serving heat the remaining 1 to 2 tablespoons butter in large skillet. Add the filled blintzes and gently brown them on both sides.

Serve at once with sour cream, berries, or applesauce.

# ⊰ CHOLENT ⊱

*Serves 8*

The origin of cholent is most likely from the pre-Inquisition Sephardic kitchen. From there it traveled through Europe and Eastern Europe. Sephardic Jews took a form of cholent from Holland to the New World where it is believed to be the origin of Baked Beans or any slow cooking bean recipe. There are hundreds of varieties of cholent. This is Patti Iglarsh's version.

*2 to 3 cups dried lima beans or chickpeas*

*3 tablespoons vegetable oil*

*3 pounds beef brisket, cut into coarse chunks*

*3 onions, diced*

*3 garlic cloves, mashed*

*2 teaspoons salt*

*1/8 cup barley*

*1 teaspoons paprika*

*2 baking potatoes, peeled and cut into quarters*

*1 pound kosher garlic sausage, cut into 1-inch pieces*

*freshly ground pepper*

*1/4 teaspoon ground ginger*

*4 eggs, unshelled*

Soak the beans or dried chickpeas in water to cover for at least 2 hours, then drain well.

Preheat oven to 350°F; if cooking overnight preheat to 250°F.

In a heavy casserole or pot, heat the oil and brown the meat, onions, and garlic. Sprinkle with salt and remove from the pan.

Place the beans and barley on the bottom of the pot and sprinkle with paprika. Top that with the meat, onions, potatoes, sausage, and seasonings. Add enough boiling water to barely cover the mixture, and place eggs in the middle of everything making sure they are covered.

Cover and bake at 350°F for 2 hours, then reduce heat to 225°F and continue cooking until the meat and vegetables are very tender.

If cooking at 250°F, place in the oven, covered, and cook overnight.

Be sure to remove the shells from the eggs before serving.

# ⚜ COLD BEET BORSCHT ⚜

*Serves 6 to 8*

8 medium fresh beets, unpeeled, scrubbed, roots and leaves removed

4 scallions, whites and a little green, sliced

1/3 to 1/2 cup fresh lemon juice

salt

3 tablespoons sugar, or more

1 large potato, boiled, peeled, and mashed (optional)

1/2 cup sour cream, or more

1 small cucumber, peeled and chopped (optional)

1 tablespoon fresh chopped dill (optional)

Place the beets and scallions in a large pot. Stir in the lemon juice, salt, sugar, and 12 cups cold water. Vegetables should be completely covered. Cook over medium heat for an hour or until beets are tender.

Correct the seasoning and remove beets from liquid. Chill the soup.

Grate the beets and place them in a separate container and chill.

Place the chilled soup, beets, and mashed potato (if using) in the food processor and mix. Add the sour cream, mixing well. Chill thoroughly.

Serve with cucumber and dill if desired. Additional sour cream should also be offered when serving.

# ⚜ CONNIE'S STUFFED CABBAGE ⚜

*Serves 6 as a main course, 12 as a first course*

1 large head cabbage

2 tablespoons oil

2 onions, sliced

3 cups canned tomatoes (from a
28-ounce can)

3 teaspoons salt

freshly ground pepper

1 or 2 beef bones with marrow

1 pound ground beef

3 tablespoons uncooked white
rice

4 tablespoons grated onion

1 egg

3 tablespoons honey, or more

1/4 cup lemon juice

1/4 cup raisins

Soften the cabbage by soaking it in boiling water or remove core and freeze overnight.

Remove 12 large leaves or 18 leaves if heads are small.

Heat oil in a deep heavy pot and lightly brown onions. Add tomatoes, 1 1/2 teaspoons of salt, pepper to taste, and the bones. Cook over low heat for 30 minutes.

Combine beef, rice, grated onion, egg, the remaining 1 1/2 teaspoons salt, pepper to taste, 3 tablespoons water, and mix well.

Place some meat mixture on each cabbage leaf and tuck sides over and roll up carefully. Place the rolls close together, touching if possible, in the sauce. Cover and cook over low heat 1 1/2 hours.

Mix together the honey, lemon juice, and raisins, add to pot and cook 30 minutes longer.

# ⊰ CORNMEAL MUSH ⊱

## MAMALIGA
### Serves 6 to 8

In her *Lexicon of Jewish Cooking*, Patti Shosteck notes that while Christopher Columbus was on his voyage of discovery, Balkan peasants were impoverished and on the move trying to locate food. Little did they realize that on his return voyage Columbus brought back with him a New World food that would ultimately benefit everyone...corn. Corn altered the diet and economic fortunes of most of Eastern Europe. "From Spain the seeds went to Venice, and the wily Venetians who actually loathed the food, unloaded it as soon as possible to the Turks in Constantinople, and from there Jewish, Dutch, and Turkish traders sold it to points as far away as Cracow and Aleppo, to Sofia and Kishinev. The peasants called the cornmeal *mamalige* (the Venetians had dubbed it *meliga*). When cooked with water it turned into filling, bland mush. But the Jews who had been expelled from Hungary and ended up in Moldavia, were grateful for any food at all and became dependent on mamalige for survival, earning them the name (from their brethren to the south) *'mamaliges.'* Eventually, more than just water was mixed with the cornmeal, and mamalige became a morning ritual."

| | |
|---|---|
| 1 1/4 cups yellow cornmeal | freshly ground pepper |
| 5 1/2 tablespoons butter or margarine | 2 large eggs, separated |
| | 1 3/4 cups buttermilk |
| 2 cups boiling water | 1 1/4 teaspoon baking soda |
| 1/2 teaspoon salt | |

Preheat oven to 325°F.

In a large pot combine the cornmeal with 1 1/2 tablespoons of the butter and the boiling water. Mix well and add salt, pepper to taste, yolks, buttermilk, and baking soda.

Beat the whites until stiff and fold into the corn meal mixture.

Grease a large casserole with 1 tablespoon of the margarine and place the mixture into the casserole.

Bake for 1 hour and 15 minutes, then melt the remaining 3 tablespoons margarine and pour over the mamaliga before serving.

# ⊰ HERRING SALAD ⊱

*Serves 4 to 6*

12-ounce jar herring in wine,
   drained
1 Granny Smith apple, peeled
   and chopped
2 cups sour cream
1 medium onion, chopped

1/2 cup seedless grapes
1 to 2 chopped hard-cooked eggs
   (optional)
1 1/2 tablespoons white horse-
   radish (optional)

Chop the herring and add the rest of the ingredients. Mix well
and cover tightly.

Chill for at least an hour.

This can be prepared a day ahead of serving.

# ⊰ KNISHES ⊱

*Makes 2 to 3 dozen*

Frances Lubkin came to the United States from Russia and was famous for her knishes. Her daughter Annice Grinberg gave me her recipe.

| | |
|---|---|
| 2 pounds baking potatoes, washed and peeled | 3 tablespoons shortening |
| | 3 tablespoons vegetable oil |
| 2 cups all-purpose flour | 1 large onion, diced |
| 1 teaspoon baking powder | freshly ground pepper |
| 1/2 teaspoon salt | |

Cook the potatoes in water until soft. Drain potatoes well and save a cup of the cooking water.

In a large bowl or food processor combine the flour, baking powder, salt, and shortening. Blend the mixture with your fingers until it resembles coarse meal. Slowly add 2/3 cup of the potato cooking water, and work mixture until it forms a ball of dough that holds together. You may not need the full 2/3 cup of water.

On a lightly floured surface, knead the dough lightly. It should be soft, but firm enough to roll. If needed add a little more flour, until dough holds a ball shape. Smooth the ball and place in a lightly greased bowl and cover with a dish towel.

In a skillet over medium heat, heat the oil and sauté the onion until lightly brown. Drain the onions and add to the potatoes. Mash them together, adding salt and pepper to taste.

Preheat oven to 400°F. Grease 1 or 2 cookie sheets.

On a lightly floured surface, roll a third of the dough into a thin rectangle about 7 inches by 14 inches. Place a strip of potato mixture about 1 1/2 inches wide along the long edge. Roll dough up like a jelly roll and cut into 1 1/4-inch pieces.

Take each piece and stretch the dough to cover the ends, unrolling dough if necessary.

Knishes should be flat on the bottom and rounded on top. Don't worry if the dough tears and the potato shows through.

Repeat the process, using remaining dough and filling.

Place knishes on prepared pans and bake for 30 minutes or until slightly browned.

If knishes are going to be frozen, bake only partially and finish baking when ready to serve.

# ↭ LENTIL SPREAD (MOCK CHOPPED LIVER) ↭

*Serves 4 to 6*

Healthy and delicious and a treat for those who love or hate liver.

| | |
|---|---|
| *1/2 cup lentils* | *1/2 cup walnuts* |
| *1 tablespoon olive oil* | *1 tablespoon mayonnaise* |
| *1 onion, chopped* | *salt* |
| *2 hard-cooked eggs or egg whites* | *freshly ground pepper* |

In a pot, boil the lentils in 1 1/4 cups water. Lower heat and simmer for about 45 minutes, until the lentils soften. Drain the lentils and let cool.

Heat the oil in a skillet and sauté the onion.

In a food processor blend together the drained lentils, eggs, nuts, and onion. Do NOT liquify—leave somewhat chunky. Stir in the mayonnaise, and salt and pepper to taste. Cover and chill.

Best if made a day or 2 ahead so flavors can marry.

Serve on crackers, party breads, or matzo.

# ⚁ MARILYN BAGEL'S BAGELS ⚌
*Makes 12 bagels*

This recipe is courtesy of my friend Marilyn Bagel, from her book *The Bagel Bible*.

| | |
|---|---|
| *2 cups warm water* | *5 cups bread flour* |
| *1 tablespoon active dry yeast* | *yellow cornmeal* |
| *4 tablespoons barley malt syrup* | *sesame seeds, poppy seeds, fresh* |
| *2 teaspoons salt* | *minced garlic or onion* |

In a large bowl combine warm water and yeast and stir until dissolved. Add 2 tablespoons of the barley malt syrup and the salt, mixing until all ingredients are well blended. Add flour and mix until all ingredients are blended.

Place dough on a lightly floured surface and knead for about 12 minutes. If too sticky, add small amounts of flour as necessary. Don't add too much. Use a sharp knife to cut dough into 12 equal pieces.

Take one section of dough in your hands and roll into a ball. Poke your thumbs through the center and work them around to make a hole a little bigger than a quarter. Repeat with the other 11 sections, placing formed bagels on a floured work surface about 2 inches apart. Be sure no cool drafts are blowing directly on them.

Cover bagels with a clean kitchen towel and let them rise for 25 minutes.

Add the remaining 2 tablespoons of barley malt syrup to 12 cups of water in a large pot and bring to a boil.

Preheat oven to 450°F and lightly sprinkle some cornmeal on a cookie sheet.

Place risen bagels in the boiling water four at a time. This is called kettling. Boil for 4 minutes, turning the bagels over frequently with a slotted spoon. If your bagels sink to the bottom and lie there, wait until they rise to the top before timing the 4 minutes.

Remove the bagels from the water, repeat with remaining bagels, and allow excess water to drain off.

Place bagels with edges touching on the cookie sheet and liberally sprinkle them with your favorite topping. Place the cookie sheet on a rack in the middle of the oven and bake for 20 minutes or until golden.

Remove bagels from cookie sheet and cool on a wire rack for 10 minutes.

# ⌁ MOCK STUFFED KISHKA ⌁

*Makes about 36 pieces*

Kishka can be served as an appetizer or an accompaniment to fish, meat, or poultry—it is almost like a stuffing. This recipe uses aluminum foil instead of the traditional cow's intestines.

| | |
|---|---|
| 8-ounce box Tam Tam crackers | freshly ground pepper |
| 1 or 2 medium onions, cut in quarters | 1/2 cup butter or margarine, melted |
| 2 ribs celery, washed, dried, and cut into large pieces | |
| 2 large carrots, peeled, and cut into large pieces | |

Preheat oven to 350°F.

In a food processor or blender, combine the crackers, onions, celery, and carrots. Add pepper to taste and the butter or margarine.

Separate mixture into 4 parts and roll into logs about 2 inches in diameter on long strips of aluminum foil. Cover logs with foil and tightly pinch the ends to seal.

Bake for 1 hour, then slice each log into 1-inch pieces and serve.

It can be frozen until ready to serve. Defrost before reheating at 350°F for about 10 minutes.

# ⛧ ROSLYN WOLF'S NO-FAIL MATZO BALLS ⛧

*Serves 8*

This recipe can easily be doubled.

| | |
|---|---|
| *3 large eggs* | *2 tablespoons ice water* |
| *4 tablespoons chicken fat* | *3/4 cup unsalted matzo meal* |
| *1 tablespoon salt plus a pinch* | *2 quarts chicken soup* |

In a large bowl, beat the eggs, add the chicken fat and mix together well.

Beat in a pinch of salt and the ice water and slowly add the matzo meal while mixing and blending everything together. Mixture will be slightly stiff, but do not add any more matzo meal. Cover bowl with plastic wrap and refrigerate 4 to 5 hours or overnight.

In an enamel or stainless steel 4-quart (or larger) pot, bring about 10 to 12 cups of water to a boil. Add 1 tablespoon of salt to the rapidly boiling water.

Using a teaspoon, take a spoonful of matzo dough and roll it very gently in the palms of your hands into a ball. Drop the ball into the boiling water. Repeat until all the dough is used up. When all the matzo balls are in the boiling water, turn the heat to medium, and partially cover the pot so the water does a slow boil.

Cook for 40 to 45 minutes and immediately put the matzo balls into simmering chicken soup using a plastic or Teflon spoon (a metal one may cut the matzo balls). The soup should be in a stainless or enamel pot to keep the matzo balls creamy white in color.

# ⚜ ROGGIE WEINRAUB'S MANDEL BREAD ⚜

*Makes 2 to 3 dozen pieces*

This much loved cookie is similar to biscotti. It freezes well.

| | |
|---|---|
| *3 large eggs* | *3 teaspoons baking powder* |
| *1 cup sugar* | *1/2 teaspoon salt* |
| *3/4 cup canola oil* | *1 cup chopped nuts* |
| *2 teaspoons vanilla* | *1/2 teaspoon cinnamon* |
| *3 1/ 2 cups all-purpose flour* | |

Preheat oven to 350°F.

Beat the eggs well and slowly add 3/4 cup of the sugar, beating well. Add the oil and vanilla and continue beating.

Sift together the flour, baking powder, and salt. Sift 2 more times.

Slowly add flour mixture to the batter, and beat just to combine. Add the nuts and shape into 2 logs 13 to 15-inches long and place them about 4 inches apart on a greased cookie sheet. Bake for 20 minutes.

Meanwhile, mix the remaining 1/4 cup sugar with the cinnamon and set aside.

Slice cookies into 1/2- to 1-inch wide pieces while hot, and sprinkle with cinnamon-sugar mixture.

Reduce heat to 325°F and bake for another 10 minutes or more, until brown and dry.

# ⊰ RUGELACH ⊱

*Makes about 4 dozen pieces*

DOUGH:

- 1 cup butter, softened to room temperature
- 8 ounces cream cheese, softened to room temperature
- 1/2 cup sugar
- 2 large eggs
- 3 cups sifted all-purpose flour (sift before measuring)

FILLING:

- 1/4 cup butter, melted
- 1/2 cup chopped walnuts
- 1/4 cup golden raisins
- 1/2 cup sugar
- 1/4 teaspoon vanilla
- 1 tablespoon plus 1/2 teaspoon cinnamon
- 1 1/2 teaspoons grated lemon rind
- 1 egg yolk mixed with 1 teaspoon water (egg wash)

In a large bowl with an electric mixer at medium speed, cream together butter and cream cheese until light and fluffy. Slowly add the sugar, beating well. Add the eggs, one at a time, beating well after each addition. Gradually add the flour with mixer on low, beating just until the ingredients form a dough. Do not overbeat.

Divide the dough into 6 balls and wrap each ball in waxed paper. Refrigerate until firm, about 1 hour.

Prepare filling by mixing together the melted butter, walnuts, raisins, 1/4 cup of the sugar, the vanilla, 1 tablespoon of the cinnamon, and the grated lemon rind.

Preheat oven to 350°F.

On a lightly floured surface roll out one ball of dough at a time into an approximately 8-inch circle. Sprinkle one-sixth of the filling over each circle, and roll up the dough into a long tube-like strip or log. Repeat with remaining dough.*

Mix the remaining 1/4 cup sugar with the remaining 1/2 tea-spoon cinnamon. Place the strips on an ungreased cookie sheet, brush with egg wash, and sprinkle lightly with the sugar-cin-namon mixture. Bake for about 25 minutes or until golden brown.

Cool the strips while on the cookie sheet on a wire rack for 30 minutes and cut strips into 1/2-inch slices.

NOTE: *You can cut the dough into triangle shaped pieces and roll into crescents by starting at the large end and rolling to the point. Place point side down on a cookie sheet and brush tops with egg wash and sprinkle with sugar-cinnamon mixture. Bake at 375°F for 15 to 20 minutes.

# ⊰ BIBLIOGRAPHY ⊱

Angel, Gilda. <u>Sephardic Holiday Cooking</u>. Mt. Vernon, NY: Decalogue Books, 1986.

Bagel, Marilyn. <u>The Bagel Bible</u>. Old Saybrook, CT: Globe Pequot Press, 1992.

De Sola Pool, David. <u>Customs of the Spanish and Portuguese Jews</u>. New York: Union of Sephardic Congregations.

Ets-Hokin, Rebecca. <u>Jewish Bulletin of Northern California</u>. Chocolate has Jewish Roots and Local Entrepeneurs.

Forristal, Linda. <u>Bulgarian Rhapsody</u>. Bladensburg, MD: Sunrise Pine Press, 1998.

Gerstl, Lorraine. <u>Jewish Cooking Secrets</u>. Monterey, CA: Millennium Publishing Group, 1996.

Gilletz, Norene. <u>Meanleaniyumm!</u> Toronto: Gourmania Inc., 1998.

Kancigor, Judy Bart. <u>Melting Pot Memories</u>. Fullerton, CA: Jan Bart Publications, 2001.

Liebman, Malvina. <u>Jewish Cookery</u>. Cold Spring, NY: NightinGale Resources Books, 1995.

Longstreet, Stephen and Ethel. <u>The Joys of Jewish Cooking</u>. NY: Weathervane Books, 1978.

Marks, Gil. <u>The World of Jewish Cooking</u>. NY: Simon and Schuster, 1996.

Nathan, Joan. <u>Jewish Cooking in America</u>. NY: Alfred A. Knopf, Inc., 1994.

Nathan, Joan. The Flavor of Jerusalem. NY: Little Brown and Co., 1974.

Nathan, Joan. The Foods of Israel Today. NY: Alfred A. Knopf, 2001.

Nathan, Joan. The Jewish Holiday Baker. NY: Random House, 1997.

Reider, Freda. The Hallah Book. Hoboken, NJ: KTAV, 1987.

Roden, Claudia. The Book of Jewish Foods. London: Viking, 1997.

Sheraton, Mimi. The Whole World Loves Chicken Soup. NY: Warner Books, 1995.

Shosteck, Patti. Lexicon of Jewish Cooking. Chicago: Contemporary Books, 1981.

# ⇥ INDEX ⇤

## ⇥ A ⇤

Almond Macaroons, 185
Appetizers, *see* Mezze
Ashkenazic Contributions
  Babka, 231
  Bagels, Marilyn Bagel's, 245
  Blintzes, 233
  Cholent, 235
  Cold Beet Borscht, 237
  Cornmeal Mush, 239
  Herring Salad, 241
  Knishes, 242
  Lentil Spread (Mock Chopped
    Liver), 244
  Mandel Bread, Roggie
    Weinraub's, 249
  Mock Stuffed Kishka, 247
  No-Fail Matzo Balls, Roslyn
    Wolf's, 248
  Rugelach, 250
  Stuffed Cabbage, Connie's, 238

## ⇥ B ⇤

Babka, 231
Bagels, Marilyn Bagel's, 245
Baharat, 43
Baklava, 186
Beans with Meat and Spinach, 121
Beet
  Borscht, Cold, 237
Blintzes, 233

Breads
  Bagels, Marilyn Bagel's, 245
  Basic Pita, 173
  Challah, Jackie Ben Efraim's, 175
  Flat, 174
  Lebanese, 177
  Matzo, 179
  Yemenite Sweet Sabbath, 180

## ⇥ C ⇤

Cabbage
  Stuffed, Connie's, 238
Cakes
  Babka, 231
  Lemon Cake, 196
  Moroccan Sweet Potato Cake,
    221
  Nut Cake with Sugar Syrup, 208
  Orange Walnut Cake, 200
  Passover Sponge Cake, 227
Carrot(s)
  and Orange Salad, 87
  Sweet, Moroccan, 163
Challah, Jackie Ben Efraim's, 175
Cheese
  Blintzes, 233
  Cheese Ball with Walnuts, 56
  Crescent Olive Puffs, 57
  Filling, Individual Stuffed Pies,
    150
  Passover Spinach Bake, 226
  Quick Boyos, 151

Spinach Bake, 165
Chicken
   Breasts with Kumquats, 98
   Circassian, 103
   Hamin, 99
   Lemon Chicken Soup, 79
   Meatballs, Grandma's, 105
   Mediterranean, 107
   with Okra, 100
   with Olives, 102
   Pie, 95
   Yemenite Soup, Tamar's, 82
Chickpeas and Rice, 142
Chocolate Salami, 190
Cilantro
   Chutney, 145
   Pancakes, 143
Coconut Macaroons, 191
Condiments and Spices
   Baharat, 43
   Hawayij, 44
   Hilbeh, 45
   Hulba, 46
   Preserved Lemons, 50
   Seven Spice Mixture, 47
   Strained Yogurt, 52
   Tahina Sauce, 51
   Yogurt Cheese, 53
   Za'atar, 48
   Zhoug, 49
Cookies
   Almond Macaroons, 185
   Baklava, 186
   Butter, 188
   Butter Ring, 189
   Chocolate Salami, 190
   Coconut Macaroons, 191

Dates in Pastry, 192
Mandel Bread, Roggie
   Weinraub's, 249
Pretzel-Shaped, 202
Rugelach, 250
Cornmeal Mush, 239
Couscous
   Sweet, 166
   Tagine, 122
Cucumber
   with Yogurt Soup, 72
   Yogurt and Cucumber
   Spread/Salad, 67

## ⊰ D ⊱

Dates
   Fish Stuffed with, 112
   in Pastry, 192
Desserts
   Almond Macaroons, 185
   Baklava, 186
   Butter Cookies, 188
   Butter Ring Cookies, 189
   Chocolate Salami, 190
   Coconut Macaroons, 191
   Dates in Pastry, 192
   Hanukah Doughnuts, 194
   Lemon Cake, 196
   Lemon Sherbet, 198
   Marzipan, 199
   Nut Cake with Sugar Syrup, 208
   Orange Walnut Cake, 200
   Passover Sponge Cake, 227
   Pretzel-Shaped Cookies, 202
   Purim Roses, 204

Rice Pudding, 206
Rugelach, 250
Sesame Brittle, 207
Dip
    Eggplant with Tahini, 59
    Hulba, 46
    Hummus, 62
    Tahina Sauce, 51
    Walnut, 66

### ⊰ E ⊱

Eggplant
    with Tahini, 59
    with Tomato Sauce, 146
Egyptian Green Herb Soup, 73

### ⊰ F ⊱

Falafel, Uli's, 156
Fava Beans, 60
    with Lemon and Garlic, 161
    Soup, 75
Fish
    Fish Roe Spread/Salad, 61
    Grilled with Chermoula, 113
    Mediterranean Fish Bake,
      Leah Perez's, 114
    Moroccan Fish with Ancho
      Chilies, David Dahan's, 111
    in Salsa, 213
    Spicy, 116
    Stuffed with Dates, 112
    with Tomato Sauce and Peppers,
      Lydia Wolf's, 115

Walnut Stuffed, 117
Flat Bread, 174

### ⊰ G ⊱

Grape Leaves
    Stuffed, 64

### ⊰ H ⊱

Hanukah Doughnuts, 194
Harira, 77
Haroset
    Abravanel Family, of the, 215
    from Turkey, 214
Hawayij, 44
Herb
    Green Soup, Egyptian, 73
    Fresh Kuku, Shou Shou's 154
Herring Salad, 241
Hilbeh, 45
Hulba, 46
Hummus, 62

### ⊰ I ⊱

Individual Stuffed Pies, 148

### ⊰ K ⊱

Knishes, 242

## ⊰ L ⊱

Lamb
  Moroccan Spicy Apricot Lamb
    Shanks, 219
Pies, 125
Lebanese Bread, 177
Lemon(s)
  Cake, 196
  Chicken Soup, 79
  Preserved, 50
  Sherbet, 198
Lentil
  Red Lentil Soup, 81
  Spread (Mock Chopped Liver),
    244

## ⊰ M ⊱

Mafrum, 127
Mandel Bread, Roggie Weinraub's,
  249
Marzipan, 199
Matzo, 179
  No-Fail Balls, Roslyn Wolf's, 248
Meat
  Beans with Meat and Spinach, 121
  Couscous Tagine, 122
  and Eggplant Pie, 132
  Lamb Pies, 125
  and Leek Patties, 217
  Mafrum, 127
  Meatballs in Dough, 129
  Moroccan Cholent, 134

Moroccan Spicy Apricot Lamb
  Shanks, 219
Sephardic Stuffed Cabbage
Spinach-Wrapped Meatballs,
  Daniela Sciaky's, 124
Meatballs
  Chicken, Grandma's, 105
  in Dough, 129
  Spinach-Wrapped, Daniela
    Sciaky's, 124
Meatless, Egg, and Cheese Dishes
  (Pareve and Dairy)
  Brown Hard-Cooked Eggs, 141
  Chickpeas and Rice, 142
  Cilantro Chutney, 145
  Cilantro Pancakes, 143
  Eggplant with Tomato Sauce,
    146
  Falafel, Uli's, 156
  Fresh Herb KuKu, Shou Shou's,
    154
  Individual Stuffed Pies, 148
  Quick Boyos, 151
  Potato and Leek Patties, 152
Mediterranean
  Chicken, 107
  Fish Bake, Leah Perez's, 114
Mezze
  Cheese Ball with Walnuts, 56
  Crescent Olive Puffs, 57
  Eggplant with Tahini, 59
  Fava Beans, 60
  Fish Roe Spread/Salad, 61
  Grape Leaves, Stuffed, 64
  Hummus, 62
  Tomato Spread, 63
  Walnut Dip, 66

Yogurt and Cucumber
  Spread/Salad, 67
Mock
  Stuffed Kishka, 247
  Chopped Liver (Lentil Spread),
  244
Moroccan
  Cholent, 134
  Moroccan Fish with Ancho
    Chilies, David Dahan's, 111
  Spicy Apricot Lamb Shanks, 219
  Sweet Carrots, 163
  Sweet Potato Cake, 221

Lentil Spread (Mock Chopped
  Liver), 244
Mandel Bread, Roggie
  Weinraub's, 249
Marzipan, 199
Moroccan Sweet Potato Cake,
  221
Nut Cake with Sugar Syrup, 208
Orange Walnut Cake, 200
Rugelah, 250
Stuffed Grape Leaves, 64
Sweet Couscous, 166
Sweet Rice with, 167
Walnut Dip, 66
Walnut Stuffed Fish, 117

## ⊰ N ⊱

Nuts
  Almond Macaroons, 185
  Babka, 231
  Baklava, 186
  Cheese Ball with Walnuts, 56
  Chicken Pie, 95
  Chocolate Salami, 190
  Circassian Chicken, 103
  Couscous Tagine, 122
  Dates in Pastry, 192
  Fish in Salsa, 213
  Fish Stuffed with Dates, 112
  Fresh Herb Kuku, Shou Shou's
    154
  Hanukah Doughnuts, 194
  Haroset From Turkey, 214
  Haroset of the Abravanel
    Family, 215
  Lamb Pies, 125

## ⊰ O ⊱

Okra, 164
  Chicken with, 100
Olive(s)
  Chicken with, 102
  Crescent Puffs, 57
Orange
  and Carrot Salad, 87
  Walnut Cake, 200

## ⊰ P ⊱

Passover
  Breakfast Fritters, 223
  Fava Bean Soup, 224
  Spinach Bake, 226
  Sponge Cake, 227
Pita, Basic, 173

Potato
  Filling, Individual Stuffed Pies,
    150
  and Leek Patties, 152
Pumpkin
  Filling, Individual Stuffed Pies,
    150
Purim Roses, 204


⇥ Q ⇤

Quick Boyos, 151


⇥ R ⇤

Red Lentil Soup, 81
Rice
  Chickpeas and Rice, 142
  Lemon Chicken Soup, 79
  Pudding, 206
  Sweet with Nuts, 167
Rugelach, 250


⇥ S ⇤

Salads
  Carrot and Orange, 87
  Fattoush, Doreen's, 88
  Herring, 241
  Jerusalem Tahini, 89
  Tabouleh, 90
Sesame Brittle, 207
Sephardic Passover

Fish in Salsa, 213
Haroset from Turkey, 214
Haroset of the Abravanel
  Family, 215
Meat and Leek Patties, 217
Moroccan Spicy Apricot Lamb
  Shanks, 219
Moroccan Sweet Potato Cake, 221
Passover Breakfast Fritters, 223
Passover Fava Bean Soup, 224
Passover Spinach Bake, 226
Passover Sponge Cake, 227
Seven Spice Mixture, 47
Soups
  Cold Yogurt, 71
  Cucumber with Yogurt Soup, 72
  Egyptian Green Herb, 73
  Fava Bean, 75
  Harira, 77
  Lemon Chicken, 79
  Red Lentil, 81
  Yemenite Chicken, Tamar's, 82
Spinach
  Bake, 165
  Beans with Meat and Spinach,
    121
  Filling, Individual Stuffed Pies,
    149
  Passover Bake, 226
  Spinach-Wrapped Meatballs,
    Daniela Sciaky's, 124
Spread
  Fish Roe Spread/Salad, 61
  Lentil (Mock Chopped Liver), 244
  Tomato, 63
  Yogurt and Cucumber
    Spread/Salad, 67

Sweet Potato
  Moroccan Cake, 221

## ⋈ T ⋈

Tabouleh, 90
Tahini
  Eggplant with, 59
  Jerusalem Tahini Salad, 89
  Tahina Sauce, 51
  Tomato Spread, 63

## ⋈ V ⋈

Vegetables and Side Dishes
  Chickpeas and Rice, 142
  Cornmeal Mush, 239
  Eggplant with Tomato Sauce, 146
  Fava Beans with Lemon and
    Garlic, 161
  Moroccan Sweet Carrots, 163
  Okra, 164
  Passover Spinach Bake, 226
  Potato and Leek Patties, 152
  Spinach Bake, 165
  Sweet Couscous, 166
  Sweet Rice with Nuts, 167
  Zucchini with Sauce, 168

## ⋈ W ⋈

Walnut
  Cheese Ball with, 56
  Dip, 66
  Orange Walnut Cake, 200
  Stuffed Fish, 117

## ⋈ Y ⋈

Yemenite
  Sweet Sabbath Bread, 180
  Chicken, Tamar's, 82
Yogurt
  Cheese, 53
  Cold Soup, 71
  and Cucumber Spread/Salad, 67
  Cucumber with Yogurt Soup, 72
  Strained, 52

## ⋈ Z ⋈

Za'atar, 48
Zhoug, 49
Zucchini with Sauce, 168

Printed in the USA
CPSIA information can be obtained
at www.ICGtesting.com
JSHW011711240424
61827JS00015B/382